Colin McCarty
Kate Ruttle

C000218413

Progress in Reading Assessment

Second Edition

Manual
Stage 2
Year 3 to
Year 6

RISING STARS
ASSESSMENT

Copyright acknowledgements

The authors and publishers wish to thank the following for permission to include copyright material in the *PiRA* tests:

Andrew Fusek Peters for the poem 'Mum' from *Sadderday and Funday*, first published in the UK by Hodder Children's, an imprint of Hachette Children's Books, Carmelite House, 50 Victoria Embankment, London EC4Y 0DZ *(in PiRA 3 Autumn)*; 'Time' © 2000 Valerie Bloom, from *Hot Like Fire*, reprinted by permission of Valerie Bloom *(in PiRA 4 Autumn)*; Lois Simmie for the poem 'Attic Fanatic', from *Auntie's Knitting a Baby*, published by Douglas and Mcintyre *(in PiRA 4 Spring)*; Geraldine McCaughrean and David Higham Associates for the adapted extract from *Crossing the Canyon*, published by Bloomsbury Children's Books *(in PiRA 5 Autumn)*; Great Ormond Street Hospital Children's Charity for 'The Pirate Crew', adapted from *Peter Pan*, by J. M. Barrie *(in PiRA 5 Summer)*; Professor Meic Stephens for the poem 'Merlin and the Snake's Egg', by Leslie Norris, from *The Oxford Book of Story Poems* (OUP) *(in PiRA 6 Spring)*.

Hachette UK's policy is to use papers that are natural, renewable and recyclable products and made from wood grown in sustainable forests. The logging and manufacturing processes are expected to conform to the environmental regulations of the country of origin.

Orders: please contact Bookpoint Ltd, 130 Park Drive, Milton Park, Abingdon, Oxon OX14 4SE. Telephone: (44) 01235 400555. Fax: (44) 01235 400454. Email primary@bookpoint.co.uk. You can also order through our website: www.hoddereducation.co.uk

Copyright © 2016 Hodder and Stoughton Ltd.
First published in 2010. This second edition published in 2016 by Rising Stars, part of Hodder Education, an Hachette UK company, Carmelite House, 50 Victoria Embankment, London EC4Y 0DZ

Impression number	10 9 8 7 6 5 4 3
Year	2020 2019 2018 2017 2016

All rights reserved. Apart from any use permitted under UK copyright law, no part of this publication may be reproduced or transmitted in any form or by any means, electronic or mechanical, including photocopying and recording, or held within any information storage and retrieval system, without permission in writing from the publisher. This publication is excluded from the reprographic licensing scheme administered by the Copyright Licensing Agency Ltd.

Cover photo © monticellllo - Fotolia

Typeset in India

Printed and bound by CPI Group (UK) Ltd

A catalogue record for this title is available from the British Library

ISBN: 978 1 471 86380 6

Contents

1 Introduction — 5
 Why use *PiRA*? — 6
 Measuring and following progress using *PiRA* — 8
 Ways in which each *PiRA* test may be used — 8
 Analysis of reading demand across *PiRA* — 8
 Thresholds for performance indicators — 10
 Who can be assessed using *PiRA*? — 12

2 Administering the *PiRA* tests — 13
 When to test — 13
 Group size — 13
 Timing — 13
 Preparation — 13
 Administering the test — 14

3 Answers and mark schemes — 15
 Marking the answers — 15
 Finding the total raw score — 15
 Profiling performance by category — 15
 Obtaining other scores — 16
 Answers and mark schemes for each test (including facilities for each question) — 17
 Record Sheet for each test (photocopiable) — 57

4 Obtaining and interpreting test scores — 61
 Summative measures — 61
 Diagnostic and formative interpretation — 67
 Reporting progress using the Hodder Scale — 68
 Predicting future performance with the Hodder Scale — 71
 Case studies — 76

5 Technical information — 80
 Standardisation sample — 80
 Reliability — 81
 Validity — 84

Appendix A: Standardised score tables — 87
 Standardised scores — 87
 Age-standardised scores — 92

Acknowledgements

A team effort led to the creation and development of *PiRA*:

- The major author was Kate Ruttle. She wrote the 14 tests from Reception year to the end of Year 4 and worked with Colin McCarty in the design, editing and evolution of all the assessments and mark schemes.
- Marie Lallaway wrote the six tests for Years 5 and 6.
- Mig Bennett wrote the playscripts for Years 3, 4, 5 and 6.
- Lorna Pepper advised on the quality and demand of all the texts and questions.
- Viv Kilburn was the language consultant.
- Jane Swift was the illustrator.
- Tony Kiek worked with Colin McCarty to undertake the statistical analyses and produce the standardised scores and target-setting predictions from the marks obtained in the standardisation.
- Colin McCarty designed the suite of tests, together with the predictive and diagnostic information for teachers, working closely with Chas Knight and Emma Rees, the publishers at Hodder, to present tests, mark schemes and information in easy-to-use forms.

Our sincere thanks go to the staff of the following schools, who administered the tests and the many thousands of pupils who took the assessments each term in the original standardisation.

Beck Row Primary School, Beck Row
Bishopsteignton Primary School, Teignmouth
Bowbridge Primary School, Newark
Chesterton Primary School, Newcastle
Cheveley C of E Primary School, Cheveley
College Heath Middle School, Mildenhall
Cranberry Primary School, Alsager
Ellington Primary School, Maidenhead
Featherby Junior School, Gillingham
Four Oaks Primary School, Sutton Coldfield
Grange Park Primary School, Enfield
Great Heath Primary School, Mildenhall
Great Linford Primary School, Great Linford
Great Wood Primary School, Upper Tean
Hambridge Community Primary School, Langport
Holy Cross RC Primary School, Catford
Horsendale Primary School, Nottingham
Lakenheath Primary School, Lakenheath
Larkholme Primary School, Fleetwood
Larks Hill J and I School, Pontefract
Lower Darwen Primary School, Lower Darwen
Malmesbury Primary School, Malmsbury
Monkfield Park Primary School, Cambourne

Much Marcle C of E Primary School, Ledbury
New Christchurch C of E Primary School, Reading
Nonsuch Primary School, Birmingham
Palace Wood Primary School, Allington
Parkstone Primary School, Hull
Pokesdown Primary School, Bournemouth
Pottery Primary School, Belper
Queensbridge Primary School, Farnworth
Sacred Heart RC Primary School, Sowerby Bridge
Scaltback Middle School, Newmarket
Seascale Primary School, Seascale
St Jame's C of E Primary School, Handsworth
St Mary's C of E Primary School, Mildenhall
St Peter's C of E Combined School, Burnham
Swaythling Primary School, Southampton
Tuddenham C of E Primary School, Tuddenham St Mary
Victoria Road Primary School, St Budeaux
West Row Primary School, West Row
Wharton Primary School, Little Hulton
Whiston Willis Primary School, Prescot
Woodside Primary School, Little Thurrock
Worlaby Primary School, Brigg
Yewdale Primary School, Carlisle

Equally our thanks go to the staff and pupils in the schools that took part in the equating study in 2015.

All Saints C of E Primary School, Maldon
Annesley Primary School, Woodhouse
Brockswood Primary School, Hempstead
Clifton Primary School, St Annes
Colmers Farm Junior School, Bolton Grove
Coupals Primary Academy, Haverhill
Glebefields Primary School, Tipton
Glemsford Primary School, Glemsford
Grosvenor Primary School, Morecambe
High Ash C of E Primary School, Great Brickhill
Kedington Primary Academy, Kedington
Langley Park Primary School, Durham
Little Hallingbury School, Little Hallingbury
Ludham Primary School, Ludham
Mapplewell Primary School, Staincross
Newton Poppleford Primary School, Newton Poppleford

North Petherwin Primary School, Launceston
Our Lady's Bishop Eton Primary School, Liverpool
Sacks Morasha Primary School, London
Sayes Court Primary School, Addlestone
St Anselm's Catholic Primary School, Harrow
St Chad's RC Primary, Manchester
St John's Primary School, Croydon
St Luke C of E Primary School, Tiptree
St Martin's Primary School, Shouldham
St Robert Southwell RC Primary School, Kingsbury
Stakesby Primary School, Whitby
Sutton Bonnington Primary School, Sutton Bonnington
Sythwood Primary School and Children's Centre, Woking
Werrington Primary School, Yeolmbridge
Woodstock C of E Primary School, Woodstock
Worfield Primary School, Worfield

1 Introduction

This is the second edition of *Progress in Reading Assessment (PiRA)*. It provides a termly standardised assessment of a pupil's reading attainment, plus a profile of reading skills, which helps you identify those pupils who may need further teaching and practice, as well as enabling you to celebrate success. *PiRA* is designed for whole-class use, with pupils of all abilities.

PiRA was designed to be used just after half-term, but may be used towards the end of each term in each primary school year in order to measure and monitor pupils' progress and to provide reliable, predictive and diagnostic information. The tests are simple and quick to administer, and straightforward to mark. Each test takes between 30 and 50 minutes, depending on the year. The tests are being published initially in pencil-and-paper format, and will be followed by an online interactive version.

This new edition retains all of the texts of the original edition, but about 20 per cent of the questions have been replaced so that it fully matches the 2014 National Curriculum and the content domain-assessable elements of the 2015 reading test framework. The new questions have been written to reflect the styles of questions exemplified in the 2015 test framework.

The tests provide thorough coverage of the new National Curriculum Programme of Study for each year. This has been assured by systematically sampling Key Stage 1 and Key Stage 2 performance descriptors for English using the 2015 reading test framework and being informed by the sample material for the Key Stage 1 and Key Stage 2 national tests.

A sophisticated equating exercise (involving over 30 schools and over 5,000 pupils) was undertaken each term between January and July 2015, to ensure that the marks pupils obtain on each new test are equated to the marks they gained on the original tests. This enables all of the age-standardised tables to match the new tests and the Hodder Scale to remain the same, and enables continuity of data for schools using the new edition of *PiRA*. Further details about this process are provided in Chapter 5 *Technical information*.

The questions in new tests have been written to be more challenging as well as using the new styles of questions, as exemplified in the test frameworks. Details of the effects of these changes are given after each mark scheme and show a similar pattern; that is, children in the equating study scored higher marks in the original *PiRA* tests and these revised, harder tests have made it possible for children to show they are doing better by obtaining higher Hodder Scale scores.

What is the Hodder Scale?

The **Hodder Scale** was developed in 2008 to provide a decimal scale that gave finer measures of progress than levels and sublevels. It was matched to levels and sublevels and has proven to be an extremely useful measure to monitor and predict progress. The Hodder Scale is now an independent progress measure. It is directly related to the raw scores in *PiRA* and does not take age into account. The Hodder Scale, as a fixed reference point, has the virtue of being a secure standard with a proven history. It is there so that teachers can use the results from a *PiRA* test, the Hodder Scale, age-standardised scores and standardised score information together with a theoretical threshold to provide clear evidence of how well children are doing with their reading from term to term.

Many teachers wish to be able to use the results from *PiRA* tests to find out if their pupils are working at the expected standard for the year and the term. This information is available beneath each mark scheme, where it indicates if a child is at, above or below the 'expected' target for that term in that year.

Why use *PiRA*?

Using *PiRA* provides many benefits to the teacher. First, *PiRA* gives reliable summative information, for example:

- if you want to follow the progress of your pupils from term to term, as well as year to year through the primary school, *PiRA* provides three carefully designed tests for each year;
- if you wish to set appropriate and meaningful targets for your pupils, and to evaluate their progress, *PiRA* tests provide an empirical basis on which to do so;
- if you need to have an external reference for your value-added requirements, PiRA tests supply it.

Second, *PiRA* also has a diagnostic capability, enabling you to investigate the strengths and weaknesses of your pupils' reading skills. *PiRA* tests give you five distinct types of information to inform you of the progress of each child, class and cohort:

- **standardised scores**, which show the standard score for a year cohort;
- **age-standardised scores**, which take into account a pupil's chronological age so that you can see how a pupil's performance compares with other pupils of the same age;
- **reading age** for a quick at-a-glance reference;
- **performance indicators**, enabling you to make a judgement against the year-related expectations of the 2014 National Curriculum;
- the **Hodder Scale**, which is an independent measure of progress throughout primary. This also allows you to compare pupils' progress in maths, using Hodder's *PUMA* (*Progress in Understanding Mathematics Assessment*).

The use of each of these scores is explained more fully in Chapter 4 *Obtaining and interpreting test scores*.

To enable you to use the information in a diagnostic/formative way, total scores can be allocated into distinct aspects of reading, as follows (see Table 1.1):

Table 1.1: Match of *PiRA* categories to the Assessment Framework domains

Reading analysis	Content domain reference
Comprehension	2b, 2c
Inference	2d, 2e
Language, structure and presentation	2a, 2f, 2g

The content domain references are provided in the mark schemes, along with the reading analysis, which defines the relevant area of the curriculum.

The balance of the questions assessing the reading categories obviously changes as the tests become more demanding, helping to pinpoint pupils' progress and alert teachers to where pupils may be underperforming.

PiRA systematically assesses pupils' reading of different text types or genres – fiction, various forms of non-fiction, poetry and playscripts – in line with national guidelines across the primary phase.

You can also examine the performance of pupils on *each question*. Using the percentage of pupils who answered each question correctly in the national standardisation (technically, the *facility value*), you can easily compare the performance of your own pupils with those in the national sample. You will find facility values by each question in the relevant mark scheme.

In short, *PiRA* will help you to answer parents, governors, inspectors or headteachers who ask:

- How has *my* child done compared to others of his/her age or year group?
- What sort of pattern of performance do pupils in a particular year typically achieve?
- Has this pupil made good progress from year to year?
- What would be a reasonable level of achievement for this pupil next term?
- What are the strengths or successes of this pupil, or the class?
- What individual and class *targets* are appropriate and realistic?
- What aspects of reading should this pupil focus on to maximise progress?
- What would constitute good, average or poor progress for this pupil or class?
- What is my child's reading age?
- If my child did a reading intervention last term, how many months progress did they make compared to the progress they made during the previous term when there was no intervention?

This manual contains everything you need to obtain a wealth of information that will enable you to be even more effective in managing learning in your classroom.

PiRA Interactive and online reporting

Using *PiRA* Interactive you can unlock even more diagnostic information. If you are using the pencil-and-paper tests, the online reporting tool on Rising Stars Assessment Online will let you analyse group performance (for example, by class and/or gender), track pupil performance through the school and generate individual progress predictions. It also provides a fully interactive option so that your pupils can take the tests on-screen, in full colour. This is then automatically marked, analysed and individual and class reports are made available.

Measuring and following progress using *PiRA*

The *PiRA* test results have been statistically linked from term to term and year to year, using the Hodder Scale, to show a clear set of information, enabling you to monitor strengths and weaknesses and track progress through the whole primary phase. This enables you to monitor and compare in detail individual patterns of performance against the norms and patterns for the term or year.

The Hodder Scale acts as a common 'spine' on which are plotted all of the *PiRA* tests across the whole primary phase (Table 4.5 on page 69 shows this scale across Key Stage 2). It provides the statistical basis for *predicting* pupil progress and future attainment, based on the termly performance data of over 15,000 pupils nationally.

Profiling test scores

The photocopiable ***PiRA*** **Record Sheets** on pages 57–60 will enable you to profile scores and analyse pupils' performance in the different reading categories. You can then evaluate their progress relative to national average performance (shown by the tints) for each aspect of reading and see if there are patterns of strengths and weaknesses. (See 'Profiling performance by category' on page 15 for further details.)

You may also go one stage further and check a pupil's individual performance on a specific question and compare how they have performed relative to other pupils in the same year group. Refer to the mark scheme to see what proportion of pupils in that year group answered each question correctly. This is called the *facility* and is shown as a percentage: 60 per cent shows that 60 per cent of pupils in the national sample answered the question correctly.

If you wish, you can also average your pupils' scores to create an overall *class* or *cohort* profile. The pattern revealed may inform both teaching and target-setting, as it will highlight the reading skills in which pupils are secure or confident and those that need to be addressed.

Ways in which each *PiRA* test may be used

PiRA provides the most useful information if it is used termly. However, if necessary, it can be used just once every year. At Key Stage 2, each test contains 40 marks and is based on varied pieces of reading material. The most important reading measures for children in the early stages of reading are decoding text and making meaning – that is, literal comprehension and language, structure and presentation. As children continue to develop as readers, inferencing becomes more prominent.

The Key Stage 2 *PiRA* tests are able to provide a profile of the core skills that underpin progress in reading, enabling you to focus your attention on supporting your pupils as they develop the most important skills for reading.

Analysis of reading demand across *PiRA*

Each test for each term has been carefully written to ensure there is a steady progression in the demand of both the reading pieces and the questions, as shown for Key Stage 2 in Table 1.2 overleaf. (Table 5.5 on page 85 shows this progression across the *PiRA* series as a whole.)

The autumn term tests are designed to be similar in demand to the previous summer term's test, to enable you to see if there has been any 'fall back' over the summer. A mark-for-mark 'raw score' comparison gives a helpful rule-of-thumb comparator to check, but reference to standardised scores and the Hodder Scale is more accurate.

To help teachers monitor the progress of their pupils from term to term and year to year, and to provide an effective way of describing and monitoring progress, we have matched *PiRA* results to our tried-and-tested Hodder Scale.

The appropriate part of the Hodder Scale is presented in Table 4.5 on page 69. It runs from 0–6+ but, for ease of reference, we have conflated the scale into three categories, to help describe the demand of the questions in *PiRA* (this is shown in Table 5.5 and 1.2 below):

- **low** covers the range 0.0–0.2 for each number on the scale (for example, 1.0–1.2, 2.0–2.2)
- **mid** covers the range 0.3–0.6 for each number on the scale
- **high** covers the range 0.7–0.9 for each number on the scale.

We have called this conflated scale the Hodder Scale of Demand. In the mark schemes, we have provided the facility for each question, which is the percentage success by the children taking the test. We have used this information to help inform our professional judgement to categorise questions into low, mid and high with the Hodder Scale to form the Hodder Scale of Demand.

The Standards and Testing Agency has published performance descriptors for Key Stage 1 and Key Stage 2 in the test frameworks, to give teachers guidelines against which to measure pupils at the end of Years 2 and 6. We have categorised every *PiRA* question taking the performance descriptors into consideration, as well as facilities and our own professional judgement to inform the balance of demand indicated in Table 1.2. This information will help teachers select tests that may be more appropriate for less or more able pupils who would find the test for the particular term too hard or too easy.

Table 1.2: *PiRA* tests analysed to show marks in each range of demand

| | Hodder Scale of Demand | | | | | | | | | | | | | | | | Total |
	low 1	mid 1	high 1	low 2	mid 2	high 2	low 3	mid 3	high 3	low 4	mid 4	high 4	low 5	mid 5	high 5	6	
PiRA 3 Autumn	2	2	0	10	8	2	11	5									40
PiRA 3 Spring		2	3	1	4	7	7	9	3	4							40
PiRA 3 Summer			1	2	2	6	9	9	6	5							40
PiRA 4 Autumn			1	0	8	6	4	4	6	7	4						40
PiRA 4 Spring				1	5	3	11	4	6	4	4	2					40
PiRA 4 Summer					2	6	4	8	9	4	2	4	1				40
PiRA 5 Autumn							4	4	12	4	8	3	1	2	1	1	40
PiRA 5 Spring								2	2	6	5	8	6	5	5	1	40
PiRA 5 Summer									3	3	3	5	13	8	4	1	40
PiRA 6 Autumn									6	3	6	5	9	7	3	1	40
PiRA 6 Spring								4	2	9	11	5	4	3	0	2	40
PiRA 6 Summer								4	4	4	9	6	6	3	2	2	40

Thresholds for performance indicators

We have provided an algorithmically derived set of thresholds that indicate where the child is with respect to the National Curriculum performance descriptors (by applying the summer standard for the whole year to a test being taken in the autumn or spring).

It is possible to set thresholds using the performance of children in the equating study, by using the facilities of the questions and applying a reasonable set of expectations, described in the table below. (Facilities indicate the percentage success of children who took the test in the equating study. A high facility indicates an easy question and a low facility a difficult question.)

This information is given at the end of the mark scheme for each test. It links the performance (facilities) to the language most commonly used to describe children's performance (for example, 'working towards', 'emerging'), based on our test-development experience.

Table 1.3: The link between performance indicators and children's success ('facility')

Performance indicator	Question facility
Working towards	90–100% success
Emerging	60–89% success
Expected	20–59% success
Exceeding	0–19% success

Our thinking behind the algorithm we use to establish the threshold for each performance indicator is: to be at the 'expected' standard of performance, children need to get all of the 'working towards' questions correct, over 60 per cent of the 'expected' questions correct and 90 per cent of the 'emerging' questions of that term's test correct, but none of the 'exceeding' questions. There is no official definition or golden rule that gives us this. However, many years of working in test development (National Curriculum tests and Optional Tests, as well as commercial tests) and analysing related data have given us the considerable experience to create algorithms to produce thresholds. The critical factor is that the rule we use has to have a sense of reasonableness, that is to say it is based on our experience, which has been informed by discussions with a number of headteachers and literacy coordinators who concur with the thinking and methodology of creating a data-driven way to evolve thresholds.

The performance indicators relate to the curriculum age-expectation for complete years. Therefore, in autumn they will be seen as very challenging and hard to achieve, i.e. any child achieving the expected standard in autumn will be doing very well. The thresholds provide another way to monitor standards and progress besides standardised scores and the Hodder Scale.

The rules we have applied to derive each threshold are as follows. Please refer to Table 1.3 for the facility values for each performance indicator.

To be at the 'Emerging' standard of performance:

- 90% of the Working towards marks
- 60% of the Emerging marks
- 0% of the Expected marks
- 0% of the Exceeding marks

To be at the 'Expected' standard of performance:

- 100% of the Working towards marks
- 90% of the Emerging marks
- 60% of the Expected marks
- 0% of the Exceeding marks

To be at the 'Exceeding' standard of performance i.e. working at greater depth:

- 100% of the Working towards marks
- 100% of the Emerging marks
- 90% of the Expected marks
- 60% of the Exceeding marks

We carried out an **equating study** to enable us to update the original tables of the Hodder Scale, age-standardised scores and reading ages for the new edition of *PiRA*. Questions from the first edition that did not relate to the new curriculum have been replaced, to ensure that every test is suitable for the appropriate term and year of the 2014 National Curriculum and the content domain assessable elements of the reading test framework.

Once we had revised the questions, we undertook a series of termly equating trials in 2015, in which over 750 children in every year group took the original *PiRA* test along with the replacement questions. The original *PiRA* questions that were kept acted as an anchor to equate pupils' raw scores (marks) in the new tests to their raw scores in the original test and so enabled us to update all the tables. (These were called the *common internal anchor questions*.) We have also increased the difficulty of the tests, in order to ensure there are enough challenging questions to provide sufficient evidence that a child is reaching or exceeding the year-based 'age-related' expectations. Whilst there has not been any major shift in demand on reading in the new curriculum compared to the previous one, the new questions have been written to reflect the styles of questions exemplified in the test framework, so that children taking the *PiRA* tests will encounter all new styles of questions. Inspection of the 2016 exemplification material suggests that questions will be more searching, and we have provided some questions that should give children practice in these styles of question.

Let's give you an example to help explain this. In any original test a raw score (for example, 20) will link to a decimal number on the Hodder Scale and a reading age and age-standardised score. The raw score the child gets in this new edition's slightly harder test may be lower (for example, it could be 18). It will therefore be this value of 18 that will now produce the same Hodder Scale score, age-standardised score and reading age. Thus, the results using the Hodder Scale and tables remain consistent and may be related back to tests taken in earlier years. This enables teachers to compare performance between the old and new editions of *PiRA*. The new tests have the advantage of being marginally harder, and so enable better differentiation of the demanding aspects of reading. This is in line with the DfE's indications that children should be doing better from 2014 onwards as the new curriculum beds in.

Who can be assessed using *PiRA*?

The spread of demand of the tests – as shown in Table 1.2 on page 9 – allows you to use each test with wide-ability groups, including weaker readers, and allows all pupils to experience some success.

Very poor readers may benefit from taking tests intended for earlier terms or years, where they are more likely to experience success and be able to demonstrate what they know and understand, rather than struggle with texts that are too demanding for them. (A number of schools in the original standardisation adopted this policy.) Table 1.2 shows the pattern of demand of each test, which you can use to select a test that should allow the poorer reader some success and yet still meet some questions that will challenge him or her. In a similar way, able pupils following an accelerated pathway may take tests intended for older age groups, which will provide evidence of them working at greater depth as they will meet more advanced texts and harder questions.

Please note that it may not be possible to obtain an age-standardised score or percentile when the tests are used in this way, if the pupil is outside the chronological age range of the conversion table for the test used. You may be able to get a reading age, and will be able to get a Hodder Scale score.

2 Administering the *PiRA* tests

When to test

The *PiRA* tests should ideally be used just before or shortly after the relevant half-term, since this exactly mirrors the time they were taken in the trialling and will therefore give the most dependable data. However, in practice, using the tests one or two months either side of this 'optimum' point is unlikely to be critical. This pattern also provides objective information for the pupil-progress meetings and data-collection points most schools have at around half-term.

Clearly, using the *PiRA* tests earlier rather than later in the second half of term can help the results to feed into and inform classroom practice or be used for end-of-term reporting.

Group size

You can administer the tests to whole classes or large groups if you feel comfortable doing so, but with weaker Year 3 children it may be better with small groups supported by a teaching assistant. In the Year 3 standardisation, some teachers found it more effective to work with small groups – say five or six children of similar ability – so that a break could be taken if required. In Year 4 onwards, whole classes may be tested together unless a child is a very weak reader – then support from a teaching assistant may be helpful, working with an individual or with a small group of similar ability children.

Timing

A maximum time limit of 50 minutes is set for the tests. In practice, in all years, the time is likely to be less than 40 minutes for most pupils, unless they are particularly slow readers or hesitant pupils.

Preparation

Each pupil will need the appropriate test booklet plus a pencil or pen and an eraser. Answers may be altered by crossing or rubbing out.

Before the test, explain the following key points to pupils.

- Tell pupils that they will be reading a number of *short* stories, poems and non-fiction texts, and answering questions about them.

- In Years 4, 5 and 6 they should *gently* pull out the centre pages, as these form the reading booklet.

- Only in Year 3 do the questions follow the section of text: the questions are embedded in the stories and information, so that pupils will not be required to hunt through the text for answers. Also, in Year 3, the first few questions on pages 2 and 3 may be read aloud, and you are advised to do this for the autumn test in particular. Everything else, pupils should read for themselves.

- They should do their best to try to answer *all* the questions.

- Explain that there will be some sections they can do easily, but that the test tends to get harder towards the end.

- They should not worry if they find some questions difficult, but just try their best and move on to see if they can answer some of the following questions.

Administering the test

Give each pupil a test booklet. Ask them to write their names on the front cover. The other information can be supplied by the teacher or teaching assistant when marking the test.

If any pupils are not clear about what they have to do, you may give additional explanation to help them understand the requirements of the test, but do not read any of the actual questions, unless it is indicated they are to be mediated by a teacher or teaching assistant. Do not help with individual words.

If the results are to be reliable, it is important that the pupils work alone, without copying from each other or discussing their answers. Remind pupils of this if necessary.

pira

3 Answers and mark scheme

Once the pupil has completed a *PiRA* test, their answers may be marked using the answers and mark schemes found in this chapter.

Marking the answers

- Use the score box in the right-hand margin alongside each question in the test booklets to record marks.
- Follow the mark scheme carefully– some questions have more than one part, or attract more than one mark.
- Please use your professional judgement when marking, recognising that children often write more words than the brief, crisp answers given in the mark scheme.
- Capital letters are not required unless specifically stated in the mark scheme.
- Do not penalise spelling: as long as the meaning is clear, always award the mark.
- Where a question asks for, say, three answers ticked and a pupil ticks four, deduct one mark.
- For scores to be valid, you should *not* award half-marks.

Finding the total raw score

You can record total marks for the page at the bottom of each page in the test booklets. Then add together the page scores to find each pupil's total raw score and record this on the front cover.

Profiling performance by category

A code beneath each mark box indicates the reading category the question focuses on. (We have used the abbreviations 'comp' for comprehension – literal understanding and retrieval from text; 'inf' for making inference – including prediction from text; and 'lsp' for language, structure and presentation – understanding structure and purpose of text.)

If you wish to profile the pupil's performance, add up the number of correct answers the pupil has obtained in each coded category and record these in the boxes at the bottom of the grid on the front cover. You can then compare the pupil's performance to the national averages from the equating study, which are provided in a table beneath the mark scheme for each test. (Note: Any small differences in averages between the text type and reading analysis are the result of rounding effects.)

You can make a visual record of the pupil's progress by transferring the category scores to the photocopiable Record Sheets, which take the form of a bar chart (pages 57–60). The national averages are shown in tints on each bar of the chart, so that you can compare the performance of a child or of the class against them.

Obtaining other scores

Refer to the appropriate tables in this manual to obtain the standardised score, age-standardised score, reading age, Hodder Scale score and performance indicator for each pupil. You can then enter each pupil's scores on the photocopiable Record Sheet. Alternatively, you can use the *PiRA* Scorer/Profiler, when published, to convert scores and generate *PiRA's* range of reporting, including performance and diagnostic analysis plus predictive scores.

In the tables beneath each term's mark scheme we have provided information about children's performance in the original edition of *PiRA* from the 2010 standardisation and in the 2015 equating study, for comparison purposes. There is also a breakdown of the overall mark by type of text, together with a breakdown of marks for comprehension, inference, and language structure and presentation, to match the content domains of the new test framework. The mark schemes also include the facility for each question. This shows the percentage success on every question by children in the equating study. All this information provides teachers with data to help them investigate a child's results.

In addition, the case studies in Chapter 4 show how teachers have been able to use this information along with standardised scores and the Hodder Scale to inform their teaching. Do be aware though that each of these measurement scales provides independent information and at times there will be differences between them, as they are generated using different methods. When they do give differing information this alerts teachers to investigate further, as it may be that a child has a patchy performance and that this is affecting the analyses.

Answers and mark scheme: PiRA 3 Autumn

No.	Answer	Mark	Content domain reference	Reading analysis	Facility %
	Keeping Pets				
1	cow	1	2b	comp	82
2	responsibility	1	2c	comp	37
3	given water to drink	1	2a	lsp	76
4	*Any one from:* Rabbits, Hamsters and Guinea Pigs Cats and Kittens Dogs and Puppies *Initial capital letters not necessary for the mark.*	1	2f	lsp	66
5	KEEPING PETS *Accept words in lower case.*	1	2f	lsp	49
6	to show what each part of the text is about	1	2f	lsp	76
7	cats (*do not accept* kitten)	1	2b	comp	61
8	rabbit ⟶ faithful pet hamster ⤬ lives outside dog ⟶ sleeps during day *All required for the mark.*	1	2b	comp	75
9	scratch	1	2b	comp	84
10	She thinks some animals make good pets.	1	2d	inf	78
11	statements	1	2f	lsp	31
12(a)	*perfect*	1	2a	lsp	48
12(b)	a dog (*accept* dogs)	1	2b	comp	68
13	A cat is a loving pet. A dog is a faithful but expensive pet. *1 mark for both correct.*	1	2b	comp	29
14	a farm *or* farms *Do not accept* field *or* outside.	1	2b	comp	55
	total	**15**			
	Billy's Tooth				
15	Billy's tooth (*accept* Billy's loose tooth) *Apostrophe and capital letter not required.*	1	2c	comp	84
16	My tooth is loose. *These four and no other words should be circled.*	1	2f	lsp	46
17	Billy's teacher	1	2d	inf	77
18	Because he had lost his tooth.	1	2c	comp	77
19	I won't have to hear about your loose tooth anymore!	1	2e	inf	69
	Was Jason hurt?	1	2e	inf	45

No.	Answer	Mark	Content domain reference	Reading analysis	Facility %
20	*Any one from:* fell out came out was knocked out *(accept phonetic spelling)* he lost it	1	2d	inf	85
21	his tooth	1	2d	inf	89
22	He wanted to show how hard they crashed.	1	2f	lsp	55
23	creeping or creeping up *(no other words circled)*	1	2g	lsp	47
24	They wanted to help. They wanted to see what was happening.	1 1	2d 2d	inf inf	67 71
25	Billy	1	2d	inf	68
26	Because Mrs Williams is fed up with Billy talking about his tooth.	1	2f	lsp	73
27	Jason was creeping up on Billy. 3 Billy was 'It'. 1 Billy and Jason crashed. 4 Billy sat behind a bush to get his breath back. 2 *Award 2 marks for all four correct;* *1 mark for any two correct.*	1 1	2c 2c	comp comp	49 39
28	Billy has lost his tooth.	1	2c	comp	22
	total	**17**			
Mum					
29	has rhymes has short lines	1 1	2f 2f	lsp lsp	66 37
30	glum chum	1 1	2f 2f	lsp lsp	73 70
31	eats the chocolate usually *Accept* eats *or* likes chocolate. *Do not accept* shares chocolate.	1	2d	inf	5
32	pause	1	2f	lsp	43
33	makes things that were wrong alright again makes us feel better when we're hurt	1 1	2g 2g	lsp lsp	43 58
	total	**8**			
	Overall	**40**			

PiRA 3 Autumn analysis of performance by category

	Questions	Marks	Average mark for 2nd edition test (2015 equating study)	Average mark for 1st edition test (2015 equating study)	Average mark for 1st edition test (2009 standardisation)
Text type					
Non-fiction	1–14	15	9.3		
Story	15–28	17	9.8		
Poem	29–33	8	3.6		
Total		**40**	**22.7**	**27.3**	**22.6**
Reading analysis					
Comprehension		13	7.7		
Making inference		10	6.3		
Language, structure and presentation		17	8.8		

Performance indicator thresholds, derived from question difficulty

Raw score	Performance indicator	Facility	Number of questions at this facility
1–13	Working towards	90–100%	0
14–29	Emerging	60–89%	22
30–37	Expected	20–59%	17
38–40	Exceeding	0–19%	1

No.	Answer	Mark	Content domain reference	Reading analysis	Facility %
	Family Snapshot				
1(a)	Family Snapshot *Capital letters not required for the mark.*	1	2f	lsp	95
1(b)	Anna	1	2f	lsp	83
2	Jane complains.	1	2e	inf	49
	Joan moans.	1	2e	inf	51
3	because it was a family birthday party	1	2d	inf	79
4	*From left to right:* Jill (*accept* aunt, *do not accept* sister) Anna (*accept* me *or* the writer) Dad (*accept* Blake *or* father) Pappy (*accept* Grandpa) *1 mark for three or four correct.*	1	2c	comp	53
5	<table><tr><td></td><td>Yes</td><td>No</td></tr><tr><td>Aunt Joan</td><td></td><td>✓</td></tr><tr><td>Grandpa</td><td>✓</td><td></td></tr><tr><td>Jane</td><td></td><td>✓</td></tr><tr><td>Anna</td><td></td><td>✓</td></tr></table> *All four for 2 marks;* *any two for 1 mark.*	1 1	2d 2d	inf inf	84 57
	total	8			
	A Present for Dad				
6	*Any one from:* Dad's birthday present to buy Dad a present to buy Dad the best birthday present ever	1	2c	comp	73
7	three *or* 3	1	2f	lsp	86
8	one — buttons two — coins three — hairgrips four — mint *All correct for the mark.*	1	2c	comp	80
9	worried	1	2d	inf	69
10	Jo finds she does not want to sell her toys.	1	2c	comp	42
11	Jill – baby doll Sam – red ball Tom – mini-skateboard Zack – robot *All four required for the mark.*	1	2c	comp	80
12	realised	1	2a	lsp	57
13	"I'd like that robot please," said Zack. "How much is it?" *1 mark if both his sentences are circled;* *no mark if 'said Zack' is also circled.*	1	2f	lsp	50
14	a kitten	1	2e	inf	74
15	unwilling	1	2d	inf	39
16	to make you read it clearly	1	2f	lsp	59

No.	Answer	Mark	Content domain reference	Reading analysis	Facility %
17	Jo had put the robot in the basket.	1	2d	inf	60
18	Jo knows what to get.	1	2c	comp	46
19	Free *Accept* Kittens *circled as well as* Free.	1	2d	inf	20
20	what she could give Dad	1	2d	inf	80
21	Jo getting a present for her dad.	1	2c	comp	69
	total	16			
	Quad Roller Skates				
22	*Any one from:* numbered list sub-heading	1	2f	lsp	4
23	quad roller skates	1	2f	lsp	86
24	four *or* 4	1	2b	comp	73
25	metal strap-on skate	1	2b	comp	41
26	Later *and* nowadays *Both required for the mark; accept* still.	1	2a	lsp	26
27	speed quad — plastic plate with wheels rollerdance skate — trainer with plate and wheels plastic strap-on skate — boot with plate and wheels *1 mark for two or three correct.*	1	2c	comp	38
28	so they don't get hurt if they fall	1	2b	comp	83
29	take a tumble *All three words – and no others – must be circled for 1 mark.*	1	2a	lsp	21
30	needed	1	2a	lsp	53
31	Tells you what the text under it is about. — label A picture to show you what the text is about. — diagram Tells you what something in a picture is called. — heading bullet points	1 1 1	2f 2f 2f	lsp lsp lsp	35 44 36
32	Learning to skate is hard. The pavement is hard. *Both required for the mark.*	1	2f	lsp	36
33	People should keep safe when they skate. People should have fun when they skate.	1 1	2c 2c	comp comp	83 58

No.	Answer	Mark	Content domain reference	Reading analysis	Facility %
34	Parts of a Quad ———————— What a quad is made from. Different Types of Quad ⟋ Wise skaters protect themselves. Protective Gear ⟍ Roller skates change over time. *All required for the mark.*	1	2c	comp	50
	total	16			
	Overall	40			

PiRA 3 Spring analysis of performance by category

	Questions	Marks	Average mark for 2nd edition test (2015 equating study)	Average mark for 1st edition test (2015 equating study)	Average mark for 1st edition test (2010 standardisation)
Text type					
Poem	1–5	8	5.5		
Story	6–21	16	9.9		
Non-fiction	22–34	16	7.7		
Total		40	23.1	25.2	21.3
Reading analysis					
Comprehension		14	9.6		
Making inference		11	5.7		
Language, structure and presentation		15	7.7		

Performance indicator thresholds, derived from question difficulty

Raw score	Performance indicator	Facility	Number of questions at this facility
1–13	Working towards	90–100%	1
14–29	Emerging	60–89%	16
30–37	Expected	20–59%	22
38–40	Exceeding	0–19%	1

No.	Answer	Mark	Content domain reference	Reading analysis	Facility %
	Bees				
1	nectar *and* pollen *Both required for the mark.*	1	2b	comp	72
2	spring	1	2b	comp	91
3	The queen finds a warm dark space — to make a nest. The queen makes a bed of pollen — to lay her eggs on. The queen makes a honey pot — to drink from. *All correct for the mark.*	1	2c	comp	81
4	Two *or* 2	1	2b	comp	91
5	lays different eggs — old queen; finds a place to sleep until next spring — new queen; hatches in late summer — new queen; dies in late summer — old queen *2 marks if three or four lines correct;* *1 mark if one or two lines correct.*	1 1	2c 2c	comp comp	98 63
6	1 egg, 4 bee, 3 cocoon, 2 grub *All correct for the mark.*	1	2c	comp	68
7	To help the reader understand the words.	1	2f	lsp	70
8	Queen bees drink honey from wax pots. Grubs eat pollen beds. Worker bees bite open cocoons.	1 1 1	2c 2c 2c	comp comp comp	75 61 54
9	To show the order things happen in.	1	2f	lsp	72
	total	**12**			
	The Bike Ride				
10	*Any two from:* new (*accept* brand new) red *accept* present	1	2c	comp	75
11	annoyed, cross *and* irritated *All three for the mark.*	1	2a	lsp	4
12(a)	in the past few days	1	2d	inf	78
12(b)	(Callum had) only been out on it once. **only** and **once** *must be underlined for the mark to be awarded.*	1	2d	inf	18

No.	Answer	Mark	Content domain reference	Reading analysis	Facility %
13	limped	1	2d	inf	13
14	to show how he fell *or* was flying through the air	1	2f	lsp	16
15	collapsed	1	2a	lsp	63
16	Callum phones home.	1	2e	inf	54
17	doing his homework — worried riding his bike — bored sitting on the grass — excited *All required for the mark.*	1	2d	inf	77
18	Callum went flying through the air. 4 Callum was standing up on the pedals. 2 Callum's front wheel hit a stone. 3 Callum was feeling good about his bike ride. 1 *All correct for the mark.*	1	2c	comp	61
19	change of time change of place change of action *All three required for the mark.*	1	2f	lsp	40
20	He'll be angry.	1	2e	inf	82
21(a)	It was warm and sunny.	1	2d	inf	86
21(b)	blue sky and fluffy white clouds *All required for the mark.*	1	2d	inf	13
	total	**14**			

Three Billy Goats Gruff

No.	Answer		Mark	Content domain reference	Reading analysis	Facility %
22	playscript		1	2f	lsp	77
23	tasty		1	2g	lsp	57
24	He is trying to persuade him.		1	2g	lsp	31
25		**True**	1	2c	comp	75
	… he wants to make Little Billy more frightened of the Troll.					
	… he wants to encourage Little Billy to cross the bridge	✓				
	… he wants the Troll to eat the grass.					
	… he knows that Little Billy likes eating grass	✓				
	Both required for the mark.					
26	scared		1	2d	inf	77
27	So you will stress the word, saying it louder.		1	2f	lsp	37
28	Little Billy		1	2d	inf	45
29	admiring		1	2d	inf	21
	worried		1	2d	inf	70
30	so the actor doesn't speak the word aloud so the actor knows what to do as well as what to say *Both required for the mark.*		1	2f	lsp	15

24   Answers and mark scheme: *PiRA 3 Summer*

No.	Answer				Mark	Content domain reference	Reading analysis	Facility %
31		Little	Middle	Big	1	2c	comp	41
	There is not enough grass left.			✓				
	He is afraid of being eaten by the Troll.	✓	✓					
	All correct for the mark.							
32	Because he is tricking both the other goats.				1	2f	lsp	15
33	cunning				1	2d	inf	11
34	Bees —— Fiction The Bike Ride —— Non-fiction Three Billy Goats Gruff —— Play (Bees→Non-fiction, The Bike Ride→Fiction, Three Billy Goats Gruff→Play) *All three required for the mark.*				1	2f	lsp	52
				total	14			
				Overall	40			

PiRA 3 Summer analysis of performance by category

	Questions	Marks	Average mark for 2nd edition test (2015 equating study)	Average mark for 1st edition test (2015 equating study)	Average mark for 1st edition test (2010 standardisation)
Text type					
Non-fiction	1–9	12	8.9		
Story	10–21	14	7.1		
Playscript	22–34	14	6.1		
Total		40	22.1	25.2	22.6
Reading analysis					
Comprehension		14	9.9		
Making inference		13	6.7		
Language, structure and presentation		13	5.5		

Performance indicator thresholds, derived from question difficulty

Raw score	Performance indicator	Facility	Number of questions at this facility
1–14	Working towards	90–100%	3
15–25	Emerging	60–89%	19
26–35	Expected	20–59%	10
36–40	Exceeding	0–19%	8

No.	Answer	Mark	Content domain reference	Reading analysis	Facility %
	Another Start				
1	Lisa *Accept* Lisa and her mum.	1	2c	comp	95
2	*Any one from:* Lisa is starting at a new school. It is Lisa's first day. The headteacher always welcomes new children.	1	2d	inf	66
3	fearful	1	2a	lsp	14
4	She was trying not to cry.	1	2d	inf	82
5	She found it hard to sleep.	1	2a	lsp	46
6(a)	reading books (*accept* books or colour)	1	2g	lsp	58
6(b)	she loved reading *or* likes books	1	2g	lsp	53
7	*Any two from:* looked different to old school (*do not accept* smelt different) looked colourful looked friendly new carpet clean cupboards exciting-looking reading books	1 1	2c 2c	comp comp	45 23
8	bored children dirty	1	2c	comp	0
9	hesitatingly	1	2a	lsp	13
10	He smiled. *Accept* He asks if she is ready.	1	2d	inf	57
11(a)	she is concerned (about her mum)	1	2c	comp	2
11(b)	she is optimistic *Accept* happy	1	2c	comp	30
12	Lisa moved to the best flat. 2 Badly behaved children disrupted Lisa's learning. 1 Lisa met her new headteacher. 3 *1 mark for all correct.*	1	2c	comp	25
13	real-life story	1	2f	lsp	42
	total	**16**			
	A Day in the Life of Roger Hunter				
14	Kirsty Pippins (*accept* Kirsty) *Do not accept* the interviewer *or* presenter *or* her name.	1	2f	lsp	76
15	playscript	1	2f	lsp	71

No.	Answer	Mark	Content domain reference	Reading analysis	Facility %
16	*squirrels store … acorns* *Roger stores … words or news or information*	1	2g	lsp	27
17	*Any one from:* to show who's talking or speaking to show that two people are talking because it's a playscript *Do not accept they are initials.*	1	2f	lsp	58
18	Rule	1	2f	lsp	62
19	research stage — no hours a day writing stage — 12 hours a day handed to publisher — 5–6 hours a day plus evenings *2 marks for three correct;* *1 mark for one or two correct.*	1 1	2c 2c	comp comp	81 45
20	interviewer (*accept* presenter)	1	2d	inf	35
21	how he spends his time	1	2c	comp	62
22	My brain needs a bit of time to recover — When the story is finished By the time the story is fully grown — I want you to know that I work very hard It's very intense — I want you to buy my book It's the most exciting and scary story I've written — I am very tired *2 marks for three or four correct;* *1 mark for one or two correct.*	1 1	2g 2g	lsp lsp	80 31
23	Some of the words are in *italics*. — They are titles, which are important to the text. Some of the words are in **bold** type. — They are names of people. Kirsty Pippin and Roger Hunter have capital letters. — They give information about the people. *2 marks for three correct;* *1 mark for one or two correct.*	1 1	2f 2f	lsp lsp	82 49
24	adventure fiction	1	2f	lsp	44
	total	**14**			
	Time				
25	eyes	1	2f	lsp	63
	skies	1	2f	lsp	70
	sighs	1	2f	lsp	63

No.	Answer	Mark	Content domain reference	Reading analysis	Facility %
26	*Any one from:* *Time*'s a bird *Time* just flies *Accept* trying to catch him	1	2c	comp	49
27	a jockey a thief	1 1	2c 2c	comp comp	50 55
28	*Any one from:* She wants to show that Time is very important in the poem. She's using the word Time as a name.	1	2f	lsp	54
29	footprints	1	2a	lsp	32
30	the moon	1	2g	lsp	33
31	sad *Accept* 'with tears and sighs'	1	2d	inf	45
	total	10			
	Overall	40			

PiRA 4 Autumn analysis of performance by category

	Questions	Marks	Average mark for 2nd edition test (2015 equating study)	Average mark for 1st edition test (2015 equating study)	Average mark for 1st edition test (2009 standardisation)
Text type					
Story	1–13	16	7.6		
Interview	14–24	14	6.9		
Poem	25–31	10	3.7		
Total		40	18.2	22.8	18.0
Reading analysis					
Comprehension		13	6.0		
Making inference		5	2.5		
Language, structure and presentation		22	9.9		

Performance indicator thresholds, derived from question difficulty

Raw score	Performance indicator	Facility	Number of questions at this facility
1–7	Working towards	90–100%	1
8–25	Emerging	60–89%	12
26–35	Expected	20–59%	23
36–40	Exceeding	0–19%	4

Answers and mark scheme: PiRA 4 Spring

No.	Answer	Mark	Content domain reference	Reading analysis	Facility %
	Survival Foods				
1	ants grasshoppers *Both required for the mark.*	1	2b	comp	90
2	under logs in old nests *Both required for the mark.*	1	2b	comp	88
3	So that you know what not to eat.	1	2f	lsp	72
4	*Any two from:* brightly coloured insects insects that sting hairy insects insects that smell bad *Both required for the mark.*	1	2b	comp	59
5	You need to know which plants you can eat.	1	2c	comp	75
6	body	1	2d	inf	83
7	<table><tr><td></td><td>True</td><td>False</td></tr><tr><td>Some mushrooms can be poisonous.</td><td>✓</td><td></td></tr><tr><td>Insects can taste better if you cook them.</td><td>✓</td><td></td></tr><tr><td>Brightly coloured insects taste nice, so are safe to eat.</td><td></td><td>✓</td></tr><tr><td>All plants growing near roads will have been sprayed.</td><td></td><td>✓</td></tr><tr><td>You must not eat any berries.</td><td></td><td>✓</td></tr></table> *All correct for 2 marks; any three for 1 mark.*	1 1	2b 2b	comp comp	92 25
8	*Heading: any one from:* Survival Foods Thank Goodness there's Goodness in Bugs! Plants: Poison or Pudding? *Label:* A grub *Capitals not required for the mark.*	1 1	2f 2f	lsp lsp	79 57
9	to separate important points of information	1	2f	lsp	57
10	*Thank Goodness ...Bugs!* — alliteration rhyme *Plants: Pudding or Poison?* — simile exclamation	1 1	2g 2g	lsp lsp	57 54

No.	Answer	Mark	Content domain reference	Reading analysis	Facility %
11	Many plants are safe to eat if you follow the rules.	1	2c	comp	16
	total	14			
	Marooned				
12	delighted	1	2d	inf	67
13	bath (*accept* warm bath)	1	2g	lsp	48
	carpet (*accept* luxury carpet)	1	2g	lsp	48
14	passion fruit — plump / pineapples — prickly / mangoes — blushing (crossed matching lines) *All required for the mark.*	1	2c	comp	85
15	edging	1	2a	lsp	19
16	He wants you to feel what it was like to be there.	1	2f	lsp	76
17(a)	But what was that? *Ignore any further words written after the sentence.*	1	2d	inf	37
17(b)	He heard a noise.	1	2d	inf	72
18	*In the first part* – relaxed	1	2d	inf	77
	In the second part – scared	1	2d	inf	65
19	to send a message for help	1	2e	inf	80
20	itchy sand / sun scorching my neck / dappled sunlight / golden sand felt wonderful / chased by bears — first part / second part (matching lines) *All five phrases correctly placed for 1 mark.*	1	2c	comp	50
21	*Any one from:* desperately Frantically *Do not accept* thankfully.	1	2d	inf	50
22	The writing reflects the writer's panic.	1	2f	lsp	50
23	It frightened the writer. It sounded like an angry noise. It was a screeching sound. *1 mark for all three correct.*	1	2d	inf	39
24	adventure story	1	2f	lsp	80
	total	16			
	Attic Fanatic				
25	rats *and* alligators *Both required for the mark.*	1	2c	comp	68
26	scaly (*do not accept* furry)	1	2g	lsp	35
27	get rid of them	1	2e	inf	84
28	*ceiling* – feeling	1	2f	lsp	74
	things – wings	1	2f	lsp	66

No.	Answer					Mark	Content domain reference	Reading analysis	Facility %
29	Dad					1	2c	comp	58
30	imagine					1	2a	lsp	27
31	scared					1	2a	lsp	75
32			Verse 1	Verse 2	Not in either		1	2c	comp	13
							1	2c	comp	46
	What the poet hears in bed.		✓						
	Which creatures might be in the attic.			✓					
	What the things in the attic are doing.		✓						
	What Dad says he will do.				✓				
	2 marks for four correct; *1 mark for two or three correct.*								
					total	10			
					Overall	40			

PiRA 4 Spring analysis of performance by category

	Questions	Marks	Average mark for 2nd edition test (2015 equating study)	Average mark for 1st edition test (2015 equating study)	Average mark for 1st edition test (2010 standardisation)
Text type					
Non-fiction	1–11	14	9.1		
Story	12–24	16	9.3		
Poem	25–32	10	5.5		
Total	40		23.9	24.6	21.3
Reading analysis					
Comprehension		13	7.5		
Making inference		10	6.6		
Language, structure and presentation		17	9.7		

Performance indicator thresholds, derived from question difficulty

Raw score	Performance indicator	Facility	Number of questions at this facility
1–12	Working towards	90–100%	2
13–28	Emerging	60–89%	18
29–36	Expected	20–59%	17
37–40	Exceeding	0–19%	3

No.	Answer	Mark	Content domain reference	Reading analysis	Facility %
	Parkside Pupils' Playground Protest				
1	school *or* primary school *Do not accept just* Primary.	1	2b	comp	71
2	*Any one from:* He likes *or* plays football. He represents football. He's captain. *Accept* He is a goalkeeper.	1	2d	inf	70
3	Jill Twitter — Pupil Sarah — Parent David Brown — Headteacher Jim Parkinson — Chair of Governors *All required for the mark.*	1	2b	comp	83
4	*Any one from:* storms argues comments told suggests states	1	2a	lsp	52
5	*Any three from:* recycle paper walk to school cycle to school turn off lights make food for the birds/feed the birds *Do not accept* do all sorts of stuff.	1 1 1	2b 2b 2b	comp comp comp	77 76 72
6	<table><tr><td></td><td>No</td><td>Yes</td></tr><tr><td>Pupils</td><td>✓</td><td></td></tr><tr><td>Parents</td><td>✓</td><td></td></tr><tr><td>Governors</td><td></td><td>✓</td></tr></table>*All correct for 1 mark.*	1	2d	inf	63
7	the plan to build new classrooms	1	2b	comp	80
8	the pupils and parents	1	2f	lsp	41
9(a)	in a newspaper	1	2f	lsp	76
9(b)	There is a headline. It reports different people's opinions. *Both required for the mark.*	1	2f	lsp	46
	total	**12**			

No.	Answer	Mark	Content domain reference	Reading analysis	Facility %
	At the Airport				
10	to go to America *or* to go to his dad's wedding	1	2c	comp	71
11	*Any one from:* Airports are so boring! Jim sighed again. He wished he was at home.	1	2d	inf	82
12	An air hostess *Do not accept* babysitter.	1	2d	inf	48
13	gobbling	1	2g	lsp	66
14	Jim → looking at planes; Jim → going to America; Jim → reading. Sandy → bored; Sandy → looking at planes. *1 mark for correct three lines from Jim;* *1 mark for correct two lines from Sandy.*	1 1	2c 2c	comp comp	52 33
15	Suddenly *Capital letter not required.*	1	2f	lsp	49
16(a)	*Any two from:* scruffy crumpled dirty green *Both required for the mark.*	1	2g	lsp	67
16(b)	They make the writing more interesting. They help to build up a picture in your head. *Both required for the mark.*	1	2g	lsp	60
17	runaway	1	2a	lsp	36
18	crouching scenting danger scanning the landscape *All three and no others required for the mark.*	1	2f	lsp	27
19	Jim is trying not to look interested.	1	2a	lsp	20
20	*Any two from:* darted, creeping *or* inching *Both required for the mark.* *Do not accept* crouched *or* heading *or* hiding.	1	2g	lsp	48
21	feels sorry for him	1	2d	inf	56
22	The story is about Jim and his feelings.	1	2c	comp	62
23	Jim → boredom; Sandy → work; the young man → freedom. *All required for the mark.*	1	2c	comp	65
	total	16			

No	Answer	Mark	Content domain reference	Reading analysis	Facility %
	Whose Turn?				
24	you fool	1	2e	inf	56
25	*[jumping down]*	1	2f	lsp	67
26	no speech marks	1	2f	lsp	73
	new line for each new speaker	1	2f	lsp	63
	instructions in brackets	1	2f	lsp	61
27	Five *or* 5	1	2d	inf	54
28	unkind *and* cunning *Both required for the mark.*	1	2c	comp	18
29	Ryan and his friends get off the climbing frame. 2 Break ends. 4 Helen asks Ryan why they are on the climbing frame. 1 Mrs Lake talks to Ryan and his friends. 3 *All required for the mark.*	1	2c	comp	51
30	[to Sam] — who the character is talking to [a few seconds later] — time is passing [politely] — how something is said [pointing] — what the character is doing *All required for the mark.*	1	2f	lsp	67
31			True	False
Ryan had been thinking about the climbing frame before break.	✓	
Ryan is being unkind to the Year Threes.	✓	
Mrs Lake is not easily fooled.	✓	| *All three required for the mark.*	1	2d	inf	19
32	He thought he was being clever. He was the leader of his group of friends during this playtime. *Both required for the mark.*	1	2c	comp	29
33	Parkside Pupils' Playground Protest — changing own opinion At the Airport — giving lots of opinions Whose Turn? — changing a friend's opinion	1	2b	comp	48
	total	12			
	Overall	40			

PiRA 4 Summer analysis of performance by category

	Questions	Marks	Average mark for 2nd edition test (2015 equating study)	Average mark for 1st edition test (2015 equating study)	Average mark for 1st edition test (2010 standardisation)
Text type					
Report	1–9	12	8.1		
Story	10–23	16	8.4		
Playscript	24–33	12	6.1		
Total		40	22.6	24.1	21.6
Reading analysis					
Comprehension		15	8.9		
Making inference		8	4.5		
Language, structure and presentation		17	9.2		

Performance indicator thresholds, derived from question difficulty

Raw score	Performance indicator	Facility	Number of questions at this facility
1–12	Working towards	90–100%	0
13–28	Emerging	60–89%	21
29–37	Expected	20–59%	17
38–40	Exceeding	0–19%	2

No.	Answer	Mark		Content domain reference	Reading analysis	Facility %
	Great Escapes					
1	70 minutes	1		2b	comp	86
	2 mins 37 secs *accept 2 mins 37 or 2.37 mins* *Answers may be written or in figures, but units must be given.*	1		2b	comp	85
2	1	1		2b	comp	70
3	Buried Alive 4 Underwater 3 Handcuff Challenge 1 *Award 1 mark for all three correct.*	1		2f	lsp	71
4	He finished the escape quickly.	1		2g	lsp	64
5	skyward	1		2a	lsp	48
6	*Any two from:* immersed submerged surface pool (*do not accept* swimming, *accept* swimming pool)	1 1		2a 2a	lsp lsp	45 47
7				2b	comp	89
				2b	comp	56
				2b	comp	13

7 Statement table:

Statement	F	O
Many people watched Houdini's stunts.	✓	
Houdini was a fool.		✓
Houdini should never have attempted the stunt in 1917.		✓
The feat in 1904 was the most interesting to watch.		✓
Houdini risked death in all his stunts.	✓	
Houdini was a famous escape artist.	✓	

All six correct 3 marks;
any four or five correct 2 marks;
any two or three correct 1 mark.

No.	Answer	Mark	Content domain reference	Reading analysis	Facility %
8	1926 – submerged	1	2b	comp	72
	1904 – handcuff	1	2b	comp	81
	1908 – straitjacket	1	2b	comp	81
9	*Any two from:* exhausted panicked unconscious	1 1	2c 2c	comp comp	61 52
	total	**16**			

No.	Answer		Mark	Content domain reference	Reading analysis	Facility %
	Lucky Escape!					
10	prowling		1	2a	lsp	43
11		*1*	1	2c	comp	38
	Tiger is shot with a dart.	4				
	Waitress enters cafeteria.	2				
	Vet arrives.	3				
		6				
	Tiger falls asleep.	5				
	All in correct order for the mark.					
12	*Any two from:*		1	2c	comp	53
	Staff were immediately evacuated (*accept* evacuated *or* immediately)		1	2c	comp	45
	Vet with tranquiliser gun (*accept* armed *or* gun *or* tranquiliser *or* special dart)					
	Vet on site within 10 minutes (*accept* vet arrives quickly)					
13	she was heavy		1	2a	lsp	57
14	*Any two from:*		1	2e	inf	50
	chased		1	2e	inf	43
	attacked					
	mauled *or* injured *or* hurt *or* bit (*do not accept* knocked unconscious)					
	eaten *or* killed *or* died					
15	sub-headings ✓		1	2f	lsp	71
	quotation ✓		1	2f	lsp	58
		total	9			
	Crossing the Canyon					
16	felt like swallowing swords (*accept* swallowing swords)		1	2g	lsp	67
17	*Any two from:*		1	2f	lsp	62
	ran a long way.					
	ran for a long time.					
	ran very fast.					
	Both required for the mark.					
18	*Any two from:*		1	2f	lsp	38
	fear					
	uncertainty					
	hopes					
19	brings us to an abrupt stop, like Juan		1	2f	lsp	35
20	wide *or* big *or* huge		1	2g	lsp	57
21	*Any one from:*		1	2g	lsp	70
	he is despairing.					
	he is worn out.					
22	despair		1	2c	comp	52
	pessimism		1	2c	comp	17

No.	Answer	Mark	Content domain reference	Reading analysis	Facility %
23(a)	2	1	2f	lsp	56
23(b)	*Any one from:* impossible *or* not possible a dream pointless unlikely *or* slim *or* improbable (*accept* hard)	1	2f	lsp	42
24	top left	1	2c	comp	72
25	The girls will make a rope and throw it to him.	1	2e	inf	56
26(a)	adventure	1	2f	lsp	84
26(b)	excitement	1	2f	lsp	74
	danger	1	2f	lsp	62
	total	15			
	Overall	40			

PiRA 5 Autumn analysis of performance by category

	Questions	Marks	Average mark for 2nd edition test (2015 equating study)	Average mark for 1st edition test (2015 equating study)	Average mark for 1st edition test (2009 standardisation)
Text type					
Non-fiction	1–9	16	9.4		
Report	10–15	9	4.1		
Story	16–26	15	7.7		
	Total	40	21.2	22.9	19.9
Reading analysis					
Comprehension		17	10.1		
Making inference		3	1.4		
Language, structure and presentation		20	9.8		

Performance indicator thresholds, derived from question difficulty

Raw score	Performance indicator	Facility	Number of questions at this facility
1–10	Working towards	90–100%	0
11–27	Emerging	60–89%	18
28–36	Expected	20–59%	20
37–40	Exceeding	0–19%	2

Answers and mark scheme: PiRA 5 Spring

No.	Answer	Mark	Content domain reference	Reading analysis	Facility %
	A Small Dragon				
1	slips	1	2a	lsp	74
2	brown *and* red *Both required for the mark.*	1	2d	inf	57
3	*Any two from:* rakes needlepoint (*accept* needle) nails spiky *(Note: three have been asked for allowing for a redundancy.)*	1 1	2a 2a	lsp lsp	85 75
4	It makes the reader pause.	1	2f	lsp	62
5	play *or* make friends	1	2e	inf	47
6	shouting	1	2f	lsp	93
7	*Any one from:* bonfire soft earth smoke on the breeze *Accept* morning sun	1	2d	inf	73
8	*Any two from:* shell split colourless crystal needlepoint nails sniffs at wisps of smoke *Accept* mouth, MUM *or* open onto	1 1	2g 2g	lsp lsp	70 65
9	disgusted	1	2d	inf	43
10	Dragon hatches from the egg. 1 Dragon wants to play. 4 Dragon changes colour. 2 Dragon tries out its claws. 3 *All required for the mark.*	1	2c	comp	74
	total	12			
	The Yellow Dragon				
11	*Paragraph 1*: happy *and* lively *Paragraph 3*: sad *and* concerned *Both required for each mark.*	1 1	2d 2d	inf inf	60 55
12	*Any one from:* hungry starving sad thirsty *Accept* ill	1	2d	inf	47

No.	Answer	Mark	Content domain reference	Reading analysis	Facility %
13	to emphasise how far the dragon must fly	1	2f	lsp	56
14	4	1	2c	comp	10
15(a)	magnificent palace *or* (plumply) cushioned couch	1	2d	inf	42
15(b)	*Any one from:* stared fiercely how dare you interrupt bellowed	1	2d	inf	30
16	Rain falls and makes crops grow.	1	2g	lsp	60
17	*Any one from:* heartless unstoppable	1	2a	lsp	41
18	wings in tatters	1	2b	comp	30
	Any pair from: lived contentedly *and* chained and bound swirled and spun *and* chained and bound sailed belly up *and* chained and bound soared above the waters and the land *and* chained and bound	1	2b	comp	11
19	selfish cruel *Both required for the mark.*	1	2d	inf	66
20	tiny, fragile creatures	1	2g	lsp	28
	sorry little people	1	2g	lsp	10
21	tells of a battle between good and evil	1	2f	lsp	78
	gives explanations of nature	1	2f	lsp	43
22	to show that the story also links to today's beliefs	1	2f	lsp	53
total		**17**			

Explorer's Journal

No.	Answer	Mark	Content domain reference	Reading analysis	Facility %
23	eyes — leathery tongue — beady tail — snake-like *All required for the mark.*	1	2b	comp	80
24	getting information	1	2a	lsp	37
25	*Length:* over 2 metres (*unit required*) (*accept* 2 metres/meters)	1	2b	comp	74
	Speed: 11 mph (*unit required*) *Food:* deer *Attacks with:* claws and teeth (*accept* speed *or* striking quickly *for either*) *Sense of smell:* excellent (*do not accept* good) *Active:* in/during the afternoon *1 mark for three correct answers. 2 marks for all correct.*	1	2b	comp	36
26	compares	1	2g	lsp	55
	know	1	2g	lsp	71

No.	Answer	Mark	Content domain reference	Reading analysis	Facility %
27	*Any two from:* (a creature from) the time of the dinosaurs only 1100 left a rare experience *Both required for the mark.*	1	2c	comp	40
28	*dangerous* – report *colourful* – poem *honourable* – myth	1 1 1	2f 2f 2f	lsp lsp lsp	37 50 45
29	It is very exciting to see a Komodo Dragon.	1	2b	comp	56
	total	**11**			
	Overall	**40**			

PiRA 5 Spring analysis of performance by category

	Questions	Marks	Average mark for 2nd edition test (2015 equating study)	Average mark for 1st edition test (2015 equating study)	Average mark for 1st edition test (2010 standardisation)
Text type					
Poem	1–10	12	8.2		
Story	11–22	17	7.2		
Recount	23–29	11	6.0		
Total		**40**	**21.4**	**23.1**	**18.9**
Reading analysis					
Comprehension		9	4.3		
Making inference		10	5.2		
Language, structure and presentation		21	11.9		

Performance indicator thresholds, derived from question difficulty

Raw score	Performance indicator	Facility	Number of questions at this facility
1–9	Working towards	90–100%	1
10–26	Emerging	60–89%	15
27–36	Expected	20–59%	21
37–40	Exceeding	0–19%	3

Answers and mark scheme: *PiRA 5 Summer*

No.	Answer	Mark	Content domain reference	Reading anlysis	Facility %
	The Birthday				
1	films	1	2d	inf	91
2	swiping an imaginary sword through the air *Accept* waving his arm around.	1	2f	lsp	88
3		1	2d	inf	77
4	emphasise annoyed *Both required for the mark.*	1	2f	lsp	46
5	[in a bored way]	1	2f	lsp	48
6	pause after each word	1	2f	lsp	71
7	[waving his sword]	1	2f	lsp	49
8	listening	1	2c	comp	87
9	light-hearted	1	2c	comp	17
10	full of energy bossy selfish *All three required for the mark.*	1	2c	comp	54
11	Alice: He won't dress up, Jack. No chance. Jack: I know. I know. But I'll make him walk the plank if he doesn't. *or* Jack: You can't come. … Unless… You… Dress… UP! *Full quotes needed, but correct punctuation not required* *1 mark for each quote.*	1 1	2e 2d	inf inf	65 59
	total	12			
	The Pirate Crew				
12	*Any one from:* cut *or* carved used a knife *or* dagger scratched *or* scored	1	2g	lsp	18
13	*To include:* They were 'feared on the seven seas'.	1	2d	inf	24

For question 3:

	True	False
Dad is excited about the party.		✓
Dad has had a bad day.	✓	
Dad hopes to dress up for the party.		✓

All three correct for the mark.

No.	Answer	Mark	Content domain reference	Reading anlysis	Facility %
14	shied at — thug dainty — famous ruffian — is scared of long known — fussy (lines crossing to match: shied at→thug, dainty→fussy, ruffian→famous, long known→is scared of) *2 marks for three or four correct;* *1 mark for one or two correct.*	1 1	2a 2a	lsp lsp	89 53
15	*Any one from:* he treated them badly like serfs *or* slaves like minions *Do not accept like* animals *or* pets.	1	2g	lsp	27
16	*Any one from:* terrified bullied scared frightened threatened	1	2f	lsp	0
17	*Any two from:* hook with which he encouraged them threatening expression to his handsome face never more terrifying than when he was most polite	1 1	2b 2b	comp comp	42 36
18	<table><tr><td></td><td>True</td><td>False</td></tr><tr><td>He is obeyed by his crew.</td><td>✓</td><td></td></tr><tr><td>When he is polite, he is always scary.</td><td>✓</td><td></td></tr><tr><td>He swears all the time.</td><td></td><td>✓</td></tr><tr><td>He has a strong right hand.</td><td></td><td>✓</td></tr></table>*All four required for the mark.*	1	2c	comp	23
19	blue (iris) red (pupil) *Both required for the mark.*	1	2e	inf	44
20	<table><tr><td>Pirate</td><td>is polite</td><td>is dangerous</td><td>has easily identifiable feature</td></tr><tr><td>Bill Jukes</td><td></td><td>✓</td><td>✓</td></tr><tr><td>Cecco</td><td></td><td>✓</td><td>✓</td></tr><tr><td>Gentleman Starkey</td><td>✓</td><td>✓</td><td></td></tr><tr><td>Hook</td><td>✓</td><td>✓</td><td>✓</td></tr><tr><td>Smee</td><td>✓</td><td>✓</td><td></td></tr></table>*1 mark for each correct column.*	1 1	2b 2b	comp comp	6 5
21	about the crew 1 and 2 about Hook 4 and 5 about both 3 only	1 1 1	2c 2c 2c	comp comp comp	47 25 43
	total	15			

Answers and mark scheme: *PiRA 5 Summer*   43

No.	Answer	Mark	Content domain reference	Reading anlysis	Facility %
	Pirate Parties				
22	place	1	2a	lsp	58
23	You can sit back	1	2b	comp	53
24	<table><tr><td></td><td>**Younger**</td><td>**Older**</td></tr><tr><td>high plank</td><td></td><td>✓</td></tr><tr><td>paddling pool</td><td>✓</td><td></td></tr><tr><td>bouncy cushion</td><td></td><td>✓</td></tr><tr><td>toy crocodile</td><td>✓</td><td></td></tr></table> *All four required for the mark.*	1	2c	comp	61
25	lay out the food	1	2a	lsp	50
26	<table><tr><td></td><td>**Fact**</td><td>**Opinion**</td></tr><tr><td>All kids love treasure.</td><td></td><td>✓</td></tr><tr><td>Everyone loves to walk the plank.</td><td></td><td>✓</td></tr><tr><td>The party is indoors in the winter.</td><td>✓</td><td></td></tr><tr><td>Pin the Patch on the Pirate is an enjoyable game.</td><td></td><td>✓</td></tr><tr><td>You eat party food with your hands.</td><td></td><td>✓</td></tr><tr><td>Food preferences are catered for.</td><td>✓</td><td></td></tr></table> *2 marks for five or six correct;* *1 mark for three or four correct.*	1 1	2b 2b	comp comp	78 54
27	rhyme engage	1 1	2f 2f	lsp lsp	57 46
28	sub-headings ——— tells you briefly … alliteration ⟍ ⟋ eye-catching drawings ⟍⟋ makes it easy to contact … link to email ⟋⟍ makes the message more … *2 marks for three or four correct.* *1 mark for one or two correct.*	1 1	2f 2f	lsp lsp	84 46
29	second person informal language	1 1	2a 2a	lsp lsp	39 27
30	<table><tr><td></td><td>**Fun**</td><td>**Scary**</td><td>**Both**</td></tr><tr><td>The Birthday</td><td>✓</td><td></td><td></td></tr><tr><td>The Pirate Crew</td><td></td><td>✓</td><td></td></tr><tr><td>Pirate Parties</td><td></td><td></td><td>✓</td></tr></table> *1 mark for two or three correct.*	1	2f	lsp	53
	total	**13**			
	Overall	**40**			

44 Answers and mark scheme: *PiRA 5 Summer*

PiRA 5 Summer analysis of performance by category

	Questions	Marks	Average mark for 2nd edition test (2015 equating study)	Average mark for 1st edition test (2015 equating study)	Average mark for 1st edition test (2010 standardisation)
Text type					
Play	1–11	12	7.9		
Story	12–21	15	4.4		
Advert	22–30	13	7.1		
Total		40	19.4	23.4	21.5
Reading analysis					
Comprehension		15	6.3		
Making inference		6	3.6		
Language, structure and presentation		19	9.6		

Performance indicator thresholds, derived from question difficulty

Raw score	Performance indicator	Facility	Number of questions at this facility
1–5	Working towards	90–100%	1
6–23	Emerging	60–89%	9
24–35	Expected	20–59%	25
36–40	Exceeding	0–19%	5

No.	Answer	Mark	Content domain reference	Reading analysis	Facility %
	Letter about Kayaking				
1	No writes to them *Both required for the mark.*	1	2d	inf	86
2	rushed to	1	2a	lsp	69
3	kayaking	1	2d	inf	64
4(a)	having fun on the river	1	2c	comp	47
4(b)	hundred times more fun	1	2c	comp	32
5	*Any two from:* red-faced puffing panting	1 1	2d 2d	inf inf	71 67
6	*either* Yes … likes it *or* No … had enough	1	2e	inf	57
	total	8			
	Keeping Joe Busy				
7	**Joe** is **Danny** is 2 5 6 11 12	1	2d	inf	47
8	The boys being hypnotised by the fish.	1	2c	comp	65
9	crouched (*do not accept* concentrating)	1	2d	inf	43
10	silvery *or* silver thin (*accept* 'length of my thumb') *Both required for the mark.*	1	2g	lsp	69
11	to show speed to show movement	1 1	2g 2g	lsp lsp	64 63
12	absorbed hypnotised	1 1	2c 2c	comp comp	47 47
13	imagine them clearly understand why the boys are so fascinated	1 1	2f 2f	lsp lsp	83 67
14	to signal a turning point in the story to change the atmosphere of the story	1 1	2f 2f	lsp lsp	70 62
15	cold *If* cold *and* nervous *both circled, ignore* nervous *and award mark.*	1	2d	inf	66
16	worried	1	2f	lsp	81
17	fish *Do not accept* water ripples.	1	2d	inf	50

No.	Answer	Mark	Content domain reference	Reading analysis	Facility %
18	Danny on hearing Mum's instruction — babyish boy / frightened of him / talkative nuisance Danny as he is climbing out of the stream — panicking concern Danny finding Joe on mother's lap *either* — bored by him / predictable boy	1 1 1	2b 2b 2b	comp comp comp	33 61 62
19	Joe sees the fish. 3 Danny searches for Joe. 5 Danny scares the fish. 4 It rains heavily. 1 *All in the correct order for the mark.*	1	2c	comp	65
20	armies march	1	2a	lsp	9
21	alliteration — clay-coated stones personification — fear was suffocating simile — like needles *Any one for 1 mark; all three for 2 marks.*	1 1	2g 2g	lsp lsp	97 84
	total	**22**			

Otter Info

No.	Answer	Mark	Content domain reference	Reading analysis	Facility %
22	It was a shame that otters died. It is wrong to let dogs run free where otters breed.	1 1	2b 2b	comp comp	90 75
23	Fish is the main source of food for otters. ✓ Otters sometimes build homes in riverbanks ✓ Female otters do not travel as far as male otters. ✓ Otters sometimes use the homes of other creatures ✓ *2 marks for three or four correct;* *1 mark for one or two correct.*	1 1	2b 2b	comp comp	96 81
24	nocturnal	1	2b	comp	81
25	holt	1	2b	comp	82
26	banned	1	2b	comp	78
27	to make us aware of how threatened otters are to help us to understand how humans affect nature *Both required for the mark.*	1	2f	lsp	48
28	headings and sub-heading bullet points *Both required for the mark.*	1	2f	lsp	55

No.	Answer	Mark	Content domain reference	Reading analysis	Facility %
29	(table below)	1	2f	lsp	43

Description	Kayaking letter	Keeping Joe Busy	Otter Info
fish		✓	✓
mainly about people	✓	✓	
mainly about animals			✓

All required for the mark.

	total	10			
	Overall	40			

PiRA 6 Autumn analysis of performance by category

	Questions	Marks	Average mark for 2nd edition test (2015 equating study)	Average mark for 1st edition test (2015 equating study)	Average mark for 1st edition test (2009 standardisation)
Text type					
Letter	1–6	8	5.1		
Story	7–21	22	11.6		
Non-fiction	22–29	10	6.6		
Total		40	23.3	24.1	23.5
Reading analysis					
Comprehension		16	9.4		
Making inference		9	5.2		
Language, structure and presentation		15	8.7		

Performance indicator thresholds, derived from question difficulty

Raw score	Performance indicator	Facility	Number of questions at this facility
1–16	Working towards	90–100%	3
17–31	Emerging	60–89%	24
32–37	Expected	20–59%	12
38–40	Exceeding	0–19%	1

Answers and mark scheme: *PiRA 6 Spring*

No.	Answer	Mark	Content domain reference	Reading analysis	Facility %
	Transforming the School Playground				
1	bored	1	2d	inf	77
2	*Any two from:* study of insects *and/or* plants *or* for Science ideas for poems *and/or* writing something with Maths outdoor classroom *Do not accept* break times. *Do not accept* flowers *and* wildlife *as separate marks.*	1 1	2b 2b	comp comp	76 68
3	to make her audience think	1	2g	lsp	50
4	giving examples	1	2g	lsp	77
5	*Any one from:* not everyone likes sitting not everyone likes chatting less space for football less space for 'big' games *Do not accept* Don't want a nature garden, *or unqualified references to football or games or chatting or sitting.*	1	2c	comp	38
6(a)	On the other hand	1	2f	lsp	60
6(b)	And another thing	1	2f	lsp	41
7	1 — to introduce the idea and excite the audience 2 — to recognise other pupils may want to use the space differently 3 — to argue for more space for running games (to involve all pupils with the nature garden) *1 mark for two or three correct.*	1	2c	comp	50
8	to explain that it will be good for everyone	1	2c	comp	60

No.	Answer	Mark	Content domain reference	Reading analysis	Facility %
9	<table><tr><td></td><td>Fact</td><td>Opinion</td></tr><tr><td>Our playground has grass with a couple of football goals.</td><td>✓</td><td></td></tr><tr><td>It would be great for break times.</td><td></td><td>✓</td></tr><tr><td>The best thing … is we could all take part.</td><td></td><td>✓</td></tr><tr><td>I think there should be an area in the nature garden …</td><td></td><td>✓</td></tr></table> *All four required for the mark.*	1	2b	comp	37
10	It includes facts and opinions. It uses present and future tense. It uses 'I', 'we' and 'you' throughout. It uses persuasive adverbials. *Either three or four correct and nothing incorrect for the mark.*	1	2f	lsp	30
11	nature garden *Accept* choosing the plants *and* designing the layout.	1	2b	comp	25
	total	13			
	Merlin and the Snake's Egg				
12	not every line is a sentence laid out in verses uses poetic language *All three required and nothing incorrect for the mark.*	1	2f	lsp	19
13	*Any two from:* The night is thick as soot The dark wind's at rest The fire's low (in the grate) (The black dog) stirs and moans Dreams trouble his sleep	1 1	2c 2c	comp comp	71 65
14	dangerous private *Both required for the mark.*	1	2a	lsp	39
15	He becomes an owl *and* flies up. *Both required for the mark.*	1	2d	inf	57
16	gathered cut *Both required for the mark.*	1	2a	lsp	28
17	to increase your interest and anticipation	1	2f	lsp	73
18	*loud* – His voice one of night's alarms *quiet* – Silent and soft he flies *Precise quotations required, apart from the capital letters and punctuation.*	1 1	2d 2d	inf inf	69 66
19	*alliteration:* steadfastly searches *or* last light leans *simile:* like a little moon	1 1	2g 2g	lsp lsp	71 71

No.	Answer	Mark	Content domain reference	Reading analysis	Facility %
20	4 goes to the wood (9 finds the egg) 2 rests 1 learns and reads (3 knows what he needs) 6 swims 7 crawls (5 talks to his dog) 8 flies *1 mark for five or six correct.*	1	2c	comp	74
	total	12			
	A Lesson in Life				
21	a machine to create life	1	2d	inf	53
22	dumb	1	2d	inf	54
	primitive	1	2d	inf	40
23	to express superiority	1	2d	inf	30
24	*Any three from:* colour of the sky laser ball game speed pods turning water into a human humans are undeveloped creatures now do not walk on the ground now do not talk to communicate now do not eat food	1 1 1	2c 2c 2c	comp comp comp	54 48 37
25	The tiny human figure would stay for longer. Professor Eden would see it work. *Both required for the mark.*	1	2e	inf	31
26	The narrator is thinking.	1	2f	lsp	49
27	*exploded* – suddenly turned	1	2a	lsp	55
	riot – many colours	1	2a	lsp	57
28	engaged pleased worried *1 mark for all three correct.*	1	2d	inf	23
29	Transforming the School Playground —— real magical Merlin and the Snake's Egg —— adventurous A Lesson in Life —— historical scientific *Two lines from any negate that mark, but do not penalise other lines.*	1 1 1	2f 2f 2f	lsp lsp lsp	64 66 70
	total	15			
	Overall	40			

PiRA 6 Spring analysis of performance by category

	Questions	Marks	Average mark for 2nd edition test (2015 equating study)	Average mark for 1st edition test (2015 equating study)	Average mark for 1st edition test (2010 standardisation)
Text type					
Persuasive	1–11	13	6.9		
Poem	12–20	12	7.0		
Story	21–29	15	7.3		
Total		**40**	**21.2**	**24.1**	**23.0**
Reading analysis					
Comprehension		13	7.0		
Making inference		10	4.9		
Language, structure and presentation		17	9.2		

Performance indicator thresholds, derived from question difficulty

Raw score	Performance indicator	Facility	Number of questions at this facility
1–9	Working towards	90–100%	0
10–27	Emerging	60–89%	17
28–36	Expected	20–59%	22
37–40	Exceeding	0–19%	1

Answers and mark scheme: *PiRA 6 Summer*

No.	Answer	Mark	Content domain reference	Reading analysis	Facility %
	The Secret Caves of Cozumel				
1	Mexico seven *or* 7 *Both required for the mark.*	1	2b	comp	97
2	Mayan people	1	2b	comp	91
3	green *and* glowing *Both required for the mark. Ignore any other extra descriptions.*	1	2a	lsp	39
4	like the canopy	1	2g	lsp	70
5	enchanting — size mysterious — beauty piercing — brightness eerie — mysterious illuminating — brightness massive — size huge — size *3 marks for all six correct; 2 marks for four or five correct; 1 mark for two or three correct.*	1 1 1	2g 2g 2g	lsp lsp lsp	87 60 31
6	*Any two from:* Very few people visit them. They are difficult to get into. They are deep underground.	1 1	2d 2d	inf inf	84 51
7	You will want to tell everyone about them.	1	2b	comp	30
8	*Any three from:* hole stairs *or* steps rock ledge *or* slippery ledge ooze pool *or* water *or* green pool roots canopy stalactites light *or* beam of light (*accept* hazy light) chamber *Any three correct labels written on, linked to or by the correct position, for the mark.*	1	2b	comp	47

No.	Answer	Mark	Content domain reference	Reading analysis	Facility %
9(a)	The pool is an incredible sight.	1	2c	comp	61
9(b)	*Any two from:* enchanting blue-green pool massive, fine stalactites piercing beam of light *Both required for the mark.*	1	2c	comp	18
10	To make readers wonder what the secret is. To reinforce how special the secret is. *Both required for the mark.*	1	2f	lsp	56
	total	14			
	Can you Keep a Secret?				
11	Carmella Mrs Alonso *Both required for the mark.*	1	2c	comp	56
12	*Any one from:* Carmella *or* anyone does not hear her *or* no one can hear her. Carmella *or* anyone is not listening. Carmella *or* anyone is not there *or* behind her *or* no one is there. (*Do not accept* Carmella is not looking.)	1	2d	inf	62
13	pause *or* hesitate *Accept* stop *or* to look like she is thinking *or* take a breath.	1	2f	lsp	56
14	hurriedly dramatically noisily *All three* required for the mark.	1	2a	lsp	58
15	doesn't expect expects expects *2 marks for three correct; 1 mark for two correct.*	1 1	2f 2f	lsp lsp	73 43
16	*Any one from:* I did just let it slip. I may just have mentioned it. I was bursting with excitement.	1	2e	inf	21
17	let down 2 surprise 1 triumph 4 despair 3 *2 marks for four correct; 1 mark for any two correct.*	1 1	2b 2b	comp comp	57 37
18	adverbs in square brackets character names on the left of the page directions to show what the characters do *2 marks for all three correct and no others;* *1 mark for any one or two correct.*	1 1	2f 2f	lsp lsp	68 21
	total	11			

No.	Answer	Mark	Content domain reference	Reading analysis	Facility %
	The Man behind James Bond				
19	*Any one from:* spying secrecy	1	2a	lsp	62
20	1908 (*not just* May) Peter Sandhurst (*accept* Military Academy) 23 1953 In the Second World War or WW2 (*do not accept* 1939). *3 marks for all six correct;* *2 marks for three, four or five correct;* *1 mark for one or two correct.*	1 1 1	2b 2b 2b	comp comp comp	93 89 44
21	People acknowledged Peter more than Ian. ✓ Peter … excelled at everything Ian (also) had a talent for finding trouble *Both quotes required besides correct statement ticked for the mark.*	1	2a	lsp	13
22	manner *or* style gift *or* liking rules *or* work	1 1 1	2a 2a 2a	lsp lsp lsp	65 57 66
23	'Asked' is a polite way to say 'told'.	1	2f	lsp	52
24	2 4 5 6 *ringed* *2 marks for the correct four circled only;* *1 mark for any two or three correctly circled* *(even if one or two others are incorrectly circled).*	1 1	2f 2f	lsp lsp	68 39
25	*Any two from:* Naval Intelligence or the secret service *or* spy skills secret codes exchanging important prisoners dangerous missions gold-smuggling deep-sea exploration criminal networks *Do not accept* travelling *or* war experience.	1	2b	comp	33
26	prepare	1	2a	lsp	22
27	travel guide playscript biography (*do not accept* autobiography) *2 marks for all three correct; 1 mark for two correct.*	1 1	2f 2f	lsp lsp	71 35
	total	**15**			
	Overall	**40**			

PiRA 6 Summer analysis of performance by category

	Questions	Marks	Average mark for 2nd edition test (2015 equating study)	Average mark for 1st edition test (2015 equating study)	Average mark for 1st edition test (2010 standardisation)
Text type					
Brochure	1–10	14	7.8		
Play	11–18	11	5.5		
Non-fiction	19–27	15	8.1		
Total		40	21.4	24.2	22.2
Reading analysis					
Comprehension		13	7.5		
Making inference		4	2.2		
Language, structure and presentation		23	11.7		

Performance indicator thresholds, derived from question difficulty

Raw score	Performance indicator	Facility	Number of questions at this facility
1–10	Working towards	90–100%	3
11–27	Emerging	60–89%	14
28–36	Expected	20–59%	21
37–40	Exceeding	0–19%	2

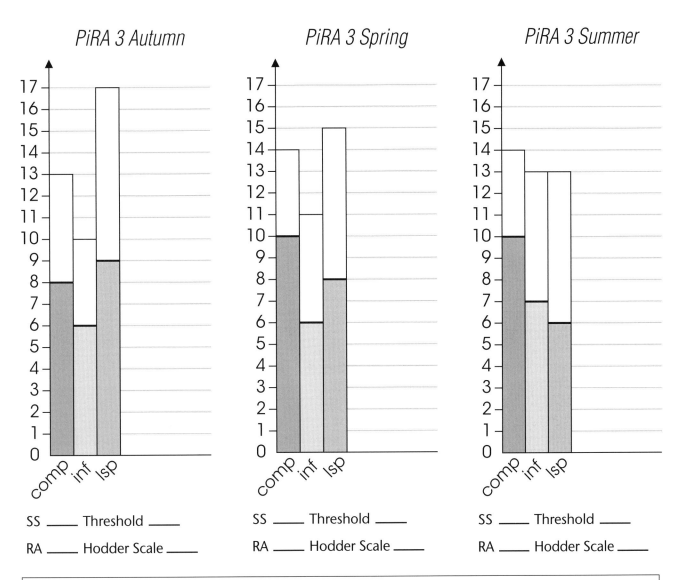

PiRA 3 Autumn

SS _____ Threshold _____

RA _____ Hodder Scale _____

PiRA 3 Spring

SS _____ Threshold _____

RA _____ Hodder Scale _____

PiRA 3 Summer

SS _____ Threshold _____

RA _____ Hodder Scale _____

Note: The tints show the national average scores obtained in the equating study, rounded to whole marks.

comp comprehension; **inf** making inference; **lsp** language, structure and presentation.
Threshold shows pupil is on track for:

Photocopiable resource: this Record Sheet may be photocopied freely.

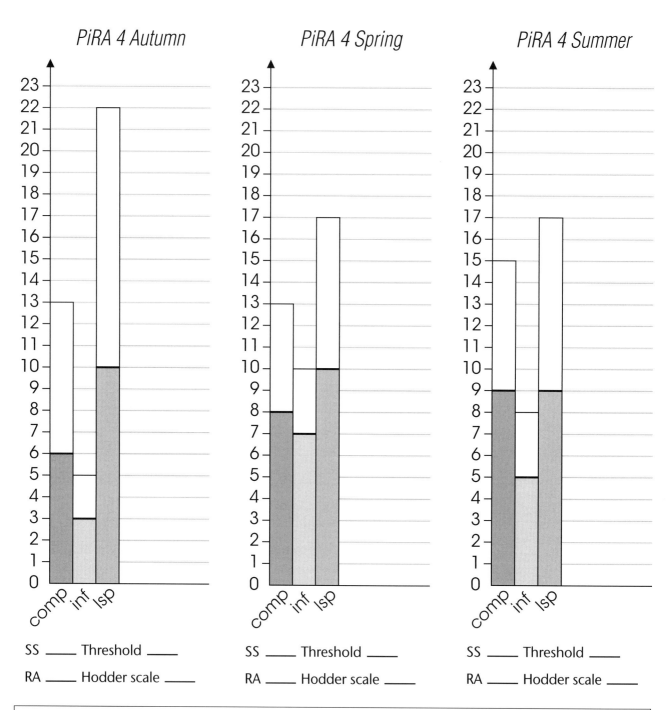

PiRA 4 Autumn

PiRA 4 Spring

PiRA 4 Summer

SS _____ Threshold _____

RA _____ Hodder scale _____

SS _____ Threshold _____

RA _____ Hodder scale _____

SS _____ Threshold _____

RA _____ Hodder scale _____

Note: The tints show the national average scores obtained in the equating study, rounded to whole marks.

comp comprehension; **inf** making inference; **lsp** language, structure and presentation. Threshold shows pupil is on track for:

Photocopiable resource: this Record Sheet may be photocopied freely.

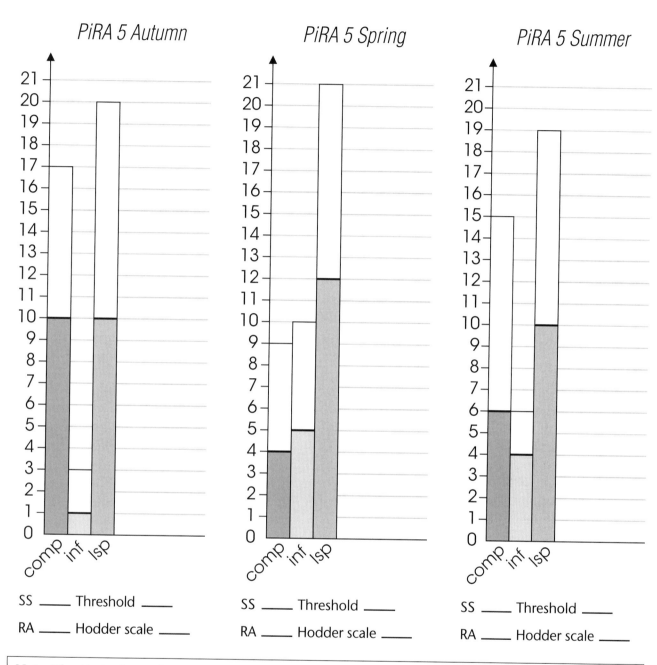

PiRA 5 Autumn

PiRA 5 Spring

PiRA 5 Summer

SS _____ Threshold _____

RA _____ Hodder scale _____

SS _____ Threshold _____

RA _____ Hodder scale _____

SS _____ Threshold _____

RA _____ Hodder scale _____

Note: The tints show the national average scores obtained in the equating study, rounded to whole marks.

comp comprehension; **inf** making inference; **lsp** language, structure and presentation. Threshold shows pupil is on track for:

Photocopiable resource: this Record Sheet may be photocopied freely.

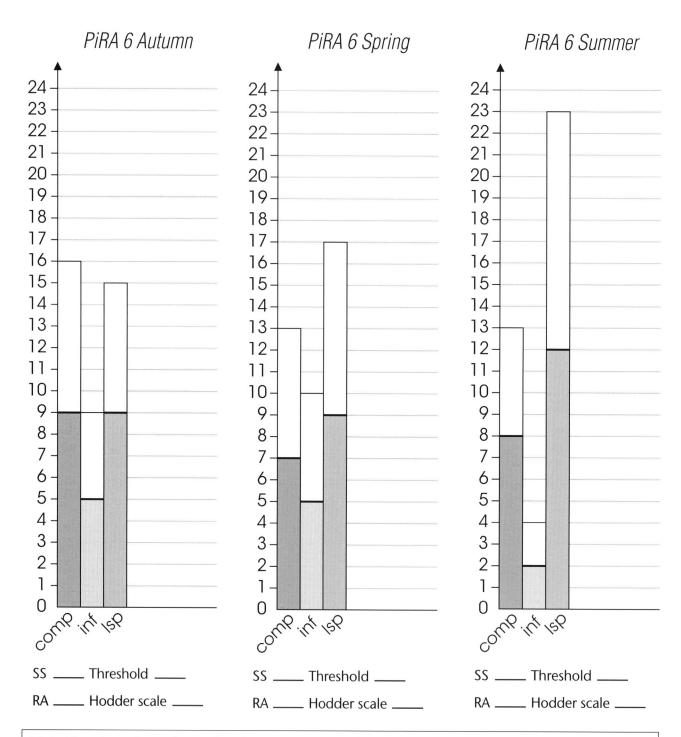

PiRA 6 Autumn   PiRA 6 Spring   PiRA 6 Summer

comp   inf   lsp

SS ____ Threshold ____   SS ____ Threshold ____   SS ____ Threshold ____

RA ____ Hodder scale ____   RA ____ Hodder scale ____   RA ____ Hodder scale ____

Note: The tints show the national average scores obtained in the equating study, rounded to whole marks.

comp comprehension; **inf** making inference; **lsp** language, structure and presentation.
Threshold shows pupil is on track for:

Photocopiable resource: this Record Sheet may be photocopied freely.

Summative measures

Raw scores

A pupil's raw score is the total mark on a particular test. As an overview, you can evaluate how well a pupil has done by comparing his/her raw score to Table 4.1. This shows average raw scores for each *PiRA* test by term and gender. You may also compare your class average raw scores to these averages, as shown in the tables beneath each term's mark scheme. In general, children did better in 2015 than in 2009/10, which is very encouraging with regard to the quality of teaching in primary schools.

Table 4.1: Average raw scores for each test by term and gender in the original standardisation

	Autumn test			Spring test			Summer test		
	Boys	**Girls**	*Total*	**Boys**	**Girls**	*Total*	**Boys**	**Girls**	*Total*
PiRA 3	20.8	24.4	*22.6*	19.8	22.8	*21.3*	21.3	24.0	*22.6*
PiRA 4	17.0	19.4	*18.0*	20.2	22.5	*21.3*	20.7	22.6	*21.6*
PiRA 5	19.2	20.4	*19.9*	17.8	20.0	*18.9*	20.3	22.6	*21.5*
PiRA 6	23.0	24.2	*23.5*	21.9	24.1	*23.0*	21.4	23.5	*22.2*

In addition, the results obtained from *PiRA* will also enable you to report pupil performance in terms of:

- age-standardised score (linked to the Hodder Scale; see Appendix A);
- standardised score (linked to the Hodder Scale, see Appendix A);
- percentile (Table 4.3 on page 65);
- reading age (Table 4.4 on page 66);
- performance indicators (see the end of each mark scheme);
- the Hodder Scale (previously known as the *PiRA* Scale; see Table 4.5 on page 69).

Age-standardised scores and standardised scores

Age-standardised scores can be used to compare how a child is performing against other children of the same age (in months) from the cohort taking the same test. For example, a child who has a *standardised score* of 100 (i.e. who is at the mean average score of the whole cohort that took the test, including both older and younger children), could have a higher *age-standardised score* of, say 110, if that child is above average for their particular age (or the converse).

Standardised scores can be used to compare how a child is performing against all other children taking the same test, that is with other cohorts of children or schools doing the same test.

Please note that age-standardised and standardised scores are quite different measures and are calculated differently. (*For example, if a class includes a significant number of younger children, then an older child could have a high standardised score, but a lower age-standardised score.*) Therefore it is not appropriate to relate a child's age-standardised score to their standardised score.

Age-standardised scores and standardised scores

Age-standardised scores

There are a number of advantages of using age-standardised scores for comparing summative performance. These include the following:

■ They are standardised to an average score of 100, immediately showing whether a pupil is above or below average, relative to *PiRA's* national standardisation sample.

■ They allow comparisons to take into account the pupils' ages: older pupils are likely to have higher *raw scores* than younger pupils, but could have a lower *age-standardised score*. This enables you to rank pupils in order of achievement after age has been accounted for. *Note:* with older pupils, exposure to teaching is likely to have a significant if not greater impact on achievement than the chronological age of the child.

Well-founded *standardised scores* (either age-standardised or standardised) can be averaged, to give an indication of the general attainment level of a class or even a whole intake. This is especially helpful when exploring school and teacher effectiveness, for it is unfair on schools and teachers to be judged as poor if they have a very weak intake, yet can demonstrate that their pupils are making good progress.

One disadvantage with age-standardised scores is that by their very nature they posit that older children will do better than younger children. In most tests, that span a number of years, this is indeed the case as age and experience does matter; however, the *PiRA* tests are written for each individual year group and our research found that in some tests age correlated weakly with performance, particularly in the spring term tests. This is not surprising as the children were all receiving a fairly common experience based on national guidelines. This common experience tended to outweigh the effect of chronological age, per se. Any differentiation in learning is not by age but by performance, so progress is likely to be, at best, weakly linked to age and reflect much more the innate ability of the child and quality of teaching, together with support and practice from school and home.

The age-standardised scores provided in Appendix A range between 70 and 130, with a mean of 100. As can be seen from the normal distribution graph overleaf, the six vertical bands determined by the standard deviation (SD) of 15 enable you to group pupils into:

■ those whose performance is within the average range (within one SD either side of the mean: 85–115);

■ those who are below or above average in this regard (between one and two SDs either side of the mean: 70–85 and 115–130);

■ those who are *well below/well above* the average for their age (between two and three SDs either side of the mean: below 70 or above 130).

For many teachers, the term *average*, based on one SD each side of the mean, is too wide and the *higher average* and *lower average* bands provide a finer set of descriptors.

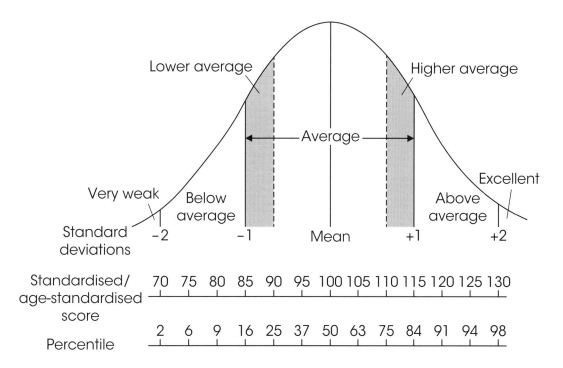

Standardised scores

Standardised scores also have a norm (mean) of 100 and a standard deviation of 15, and in many ways are similar to age-standardised scores, except no allowance is made for the age of the child. As such, the above information applies to standardised scores.

Standardised scores will be reported from the Key Stage 1 and Key Stage 2 national tests. We have included, in Appendix A, standardised scores for all the *PiRA* tests. They are useful for comparing children from one cohort to another but require that the children take the same test for this comparison to be made. (Age-standardised scores, by contrast, enable you to compare performance in any age-standardised test.) They have a limited value in comparing progress over time because they rely on the cohort being similar. In very large samples of 100,000 it may be a reasonable measure, but for smaller samples of one class this may not give reliable information and age standardisation is to be preferred. Often, standardised scores are accompanied by an independent scale that is referenced by each test and can show or monitor progress over time. We have taken standardised scores and linked them to the Hodder Scale to enable teachers to monitor progress term by term using the scale, and to predict progress too, which standardised scores are not designed to do.

A simple approach is to look up the marks and use the standardised scores (and Hodder Scale) in Appendix A and assume that all children within the range 90–110 of the mean (100) are at the appropriate standard for that term and are on target to achieve the expected standard at the end of the year.

Table 4.2: Relationship between age-standardised/standardised test scores and qualitative interpretations

Standardised score	Qualitative interpretation	Standard deviation from mean	Percentile score	Percentage of normal population
>130	Excellent	>+2	>98	2.28
116–130	Well above average	+1 to +2	85–98	13.59
110–115 85–115 85–90	_higher average_ Average/age-appropriate _lower average_	−1 to +1	16–84	68.26
70–84	Well below average	−1 to −2	2–15	13.59
<70	Very weak	<−2	<2	2.28

A danger is that age-standardised and standardised scores can give a spurious accuracy and imply too fine a distinction – suggesting one pupil is better than another, where the confidence limit of the mark does not warrant this. Care is therefore advised when placing pupils in order of merit.

The 90 per cent confidence band for the Key Stage 2 _PiRA_ tests is typically plus or minus 4 (see Table 5.3) – so for a pupil with an age-standardised score of, for example, 106 you can be 90 per cent confident that their 'true' score is between 102 and 110.

Percentiles

Percentiles can help to give you a better feel for the significance of a pupil's reading age, because they show the percentage in each age group who score below a certain level. So an age-standardised or standardised score at the 68th percentile means that 68 per cent of the group scored below that pupil's standardised score. Thus the pupil is in the top third for his/her age group.

Percentile scores may be derived from age-standardised scores. To obtain a pupil's percentile, first calculate the pupil's chronological age in years and completed months, obtain his/her age-standardised score using the appropriate conversion table at the end of this manual, and then refer to Table 4.3 overleaf. Equally, standardised scores may be used in the same way but obviously without the need to reference a chronological age.

The relationship between age-standardised scores and percentiles is most easily seen by reference to the normal distribution graph shown on page 63.

Table 4.3: Relationship between age-standardised/standardised scores and percentiles

Age-standardised score	Percentile	Age-standardised score	Percentile	Age-standardised score	Percentile
≥130	>98	108	70	89	24
128–9	97	107	68	88	22
126–7	96	106	66	87	20
125	95	105	63	86	18
123–4	94	104	60	85	16
122	93	103	58	84	14
121	92	102	55	83	13
120	91	101	52	82	12
119	90	100	50	81	11
118	89	99	48	80	9
117	87	98	45	79	8
116	86	97	42	78	7
115	84	96	40	76–7	6
114	82	95	37	75	5
113	80	94	34	73–4	4
112	78	93	32	71–2	3
111	77	92	30	70	2
110	74	91	28	<70	1
109	72	90	26		

Reading ages

Reading ages are used by many teachers as a quick reference: a reading age shows the *average* chronological age of the pupils who obtained each particular raw score – that is, the chronological age at which this level of performance is typical. However, for more detailed comparative information, and especially for tracking progress over time, age-standardised scores and percentiles are to be preferred.

Note that *PiRA* reading ages are provided for ages beyond the normal age range for a given year group. These have been generated by using statistical extrapolations, by up to six months either side of the main range of Key Stage 2 pupils taking the tests in the standardisation. Such extrapolations can be especially useful in interpreting the performance of weaker readers who have been given a test for a younger age range.

Table 4.4: Reading ages for each term

PiRA 3 raw score	Autumn	Spring	Summer	PiRA 4 raw score	Autumn	Spring	Summer	PiRA 5 raw score	Autumn	Spring	Summer	PiRA 6 raw score	Autumn	Spring	Summer
1-7	<6:5	<6:10	<7:1	1-7	<7:4	<7:9	<8:2	1-7	<8:6	<8:10		1-7			
8				8	7:4			8				8			
9				9	7:7			9		8:10		9			
10				10	7:9			10	8:6	8:11	<9:2	10	<9:0	<9:2	<9:2
11				11	7:11			11	8:7	9:1		11			
12				12	8:2			12	8:9	9:2		12			
13				13	8:4			13	8:10	9:4		13			
14	6:5			14	8:6			14	9:0	9:5	9:2	14			
15	6:8			15	8:8			15	9:1	9:7	9:5	15			9:2
16	6:10	6:10		16	8:11	7:9	8:2	16	9:3	9:8	9:7	16	9:0	9:2	9:7
17	7:1	7:0		17	9:2	8:3	8:5	17	9:5	9:10	9:9	17	9:5	9:7	10:0
18	7:2	7:3	7:1	18	9:5	8:7	8:8	18	9:6	9:11	10:1	18	9:7	9:10	10:3
19	7:3	7:6	7:5	19	9:8	8:10	8:11	19	9:8	10:0	10:4	19	9:10	10:1	10:7
20	7:6	7:9	7:8	20	9:10	9:2	9:2	20	9:9	10:2	10:6	20	10:0	10:4	10:11
21	7:8	8:0	8:0	21	10:0	9:5	9:5	21	9:11	10:4	10:10	21	10:3	10:7	11:3
22	7:11	8:2	8:4	22	>10:0	9:9	9:7	22	10:0	10:6	11:1	22	10:5	10:11	11:7
23	8:1	8:5	8:8	23		10:0	9:11	23	10:2	10:8	11:3	23	10:8	11:3	11:11
24	8:4	8:8	9:0	24		10:1	10:4	24	10:3	10:9	11:4	24	10:10	11:8	12:3
25	8:6	8:11	9:4	25		10:3	10:6	25	10:5	10:11	11:5	25	11:0	12:0	12:6
26	8:8	9:1	9:5	26		>10:3	>10:6	26	10:6	11:0	11:6	26	11:3	12:2	>12:6
27	8:11	9:2	9:6	27				27	10:8	11:1	>11:6	27	11:5	12:4	
28	9:0	9:3	9:7	28				28	10:9	11:3		28	11:8	>12:4	
29	>9:0	>9:3	>9:7	29				29	10:11	>11:3		29	11:10		
30				30				30	11:0			30	12:0		
31-40				31-40				31-40	>11:0			31-40	>12:0		

Diagnostic and formative interpretation

Summative measures are valuable, but only give an *overall* picture of the child's performance relative to his/her peers. Such data may, for example, confirm that the pupil is doing well for his/her age and indicate that no intervention strategy is required. However, a more detailed check may show, for example, that good literal reading accuracy is masking a weakness in comprehension and inference.

Using the *PiRA* profile

Use the *PiRA* profile on the Record Sheets (pages 57–60) to see if there are patterns of strengths and weaknesses in:

- Comprehension – literal understanding and retrieval from text;
- Making inference – including prediction from text;
- Language, structure and presentation – understanding structure and purpose of text.

Every pupil has particular strengths and weaknesses that will show up in the *PiRA* profile. When you examine the pupil's answers, you can see when there is a change from correct to incorrect, and at what level of demand this is occurring. This may alert you to generally weak achievement or perhaps to weakness (or strength) in one specific aspect of reading. This may highlight aspects of literacy which have previously been taught but which have been forgotten or were not understood at the time.

It should be borne in mind when undertaking this form of analysis that performance will naturally reflect recent teaching.

Check a pupil's performance on a specific question

You may also go one stage further and check a pupil's individual performance on a specific question and compare how they have performed relative to other pupils in the same year group. Refer to the mark scheme to see what proportion of pupils in that year group answered each question correctly. This is called the *facility* and is shown as a percentage: 60 per cent shows that 60 per cent of pupils in the national sample answered the question correctly.

If you wish, you can also average your pupils' scores to create an overall *class* or *cohort* profile. The pattern revealed may inform both teaching and target-setting, as it will highlight the reading skills in which pupils are secure or confident and those that need to be addressed.

Obtaining patterns and predictions of performance

The Hodder Scale enables you to predict pupils' future performance and measure whether current progress is what would have been expected, as you monitor performance from term to term.

Table 4.5 on page 69 gives the relationships between Hodder Scale scores term by term, so you can always refer a total score to this table to see what is predicted for any pupil (or class). Reading back from the Hodder Scale in Table 4.5 will give you the raw score the pupil should achieve in any future term.

The case studies later in this chapter indicate how this comparative information enables some next steps to be planned. With this more detailed picture, it is possible to implement specific teaching strategies to help both weak and good readers to improve.

Reporting progress using the Hodder Scale

In developing the *PiRA* tests, seven cohorts of pupils – 10,000 pupils – were tracked termly over a full academic year. Using this information, plus Optional and Key Stage test data, it was possible to link pupil performance from term to term and year to year, to identify patterns that provide a firm basis on which to project future performance and establish realistic expectations. The data was further strengthened by repeating the tests for Years 2 and 6 in successive summer terms, to gather an extra tier of year-on-year information with respect to Key Stages 1 and 2, and to provide a sample of over 1,800 children across these two years. Table 4.7 on page 72 draws this information together across all four years, from summer in Year 3 to summer Year 6.

The equating trials carried out in 2015 ensure that this linking of Hodder Scale scores is secure for the new edition.

The Hodder Scale score is the most useful monitoring scale, as it shows a decimalised measure of progress and enables teachers to monitor progress term by term at a much finer level than the scaling used by most commercial data-tracking programmes. It is also much more helpful for monitoring and tracking progress than merely categorising children at the expected standard for the year or above or below that standard. For example, a simple way is to look up the marks and use the standardised scores (and Hodder Scale) in Appendix A and assume that all children within the range 90–110 of the mean (100) are at the appropriate standard for that term and are on target to achieve the expected standard at the end of the year.

Table 4.5: Relating *PiRA* raw scores to the Hodder Scale

First find the raw score in the column for the test your pupils have taken, then read across to obtain the Hodder Scale score.

Years 3 and 4

Hodder Scale	Raw score						Hodder Scale
	PiRA 3 Autumn	PiRA 3 Spring	PiRA 3 Summer	PiRA 4 Autumn	PiRA 4 Spring	PiRA 4 Summer	
1.1	1						1.1
1.2	2						1.2
1.3		<3					1.3
1.4	3	3	1				1.4
1.5		4	2				1.5
1.6	4	5	3	1			1.6
1.7		6	4			1	1.7
1.8	5	7	5		<6	2	1.8
1.9	6	8	6	2	6	3	1.9
2.0	7	9–10	7	3	7	4	2.0
2.1	8–9	11–13	8	4	8	5	2.1
2.2	10–11	14–15	9–10	5–6	9	6–7	2.2
2.3	12–13	16	11	7	10	8	2.3
2.4	14–15	17	12	8–9	11	9	2.4
2.5	16–18	18	13	10	12		2.5
2.6	19–20	19–20	14–15	11	13	10	2.6
2.7	21–22	21	16	12	14		2.7
2.8	23–24	22–23	17	13	15	11	2.8
2.9	25–27	24–25	18–19	14	16–17	12	2.9
3.0	28–29	26	20	15–16	18	13	3.0
3.1	30–31	27	21	17	19–20	14	3.1
3.2	32	28	22–23	18	21	15–16	3.2
3.3	33		24	19	22	17	3.3
3.4	34	29	25		23	18	3.4
3.5	35		26	20		19	3.5
3.6	36	30	27	21	24	20	3.6
3.7	37	31	28	22	25	21	3.7
3.8	38	32	29	23	26	22	3.8
3.9	39	33	30	24	27–28	23	3.9
4.0	40	34	31	25	29	24	4.0
4.1		35–36		26		25	4.1
4.2		37–38			30	26	4.2
4.3		39–40	32	27		27	4.3
4.4			33			28	4.4
4.5			34	28	31	29	4.5
4.6			35	29	32	30	4.6
4.7			36–40	30–31	33–34	31	4.7
4.8				32–33	35–36	32	4.8
4.9				34–35	37–38	33–34	4.9
5.0				36–40	39–40	35–36	5.0
5.1						37–38	5.1
5.2						39–40	5.2

Years 5 and 6

Hodder Scale	Raw score						Hodder Scale
	PiRA 5 Autumn	PiRA 5 Spring	PiRA 5 Summer	PiRA 6 Autumn	PiRA 6 Spring	PiRA 6 Summer	
1.8		<4	1				1.8
1.9	1	4	2	1			1.9
2.0	2		3	2			2.0
2.1	3			3		1	2.1
2.2	4	5		4		2	2.2
2.3	5			5	<4	3	2.3
2.4	6–7		4	6	4		2.4
2.5	8			7			2.5
2.6	9	6	5	8	5	4	2.6
2.7			6	9–10		5	2.7
2.8	10	7	7	11	6	6	2.8
2.9	11	8–9	8	12	7	7	2.9
3.0	12	10	9		8		3.0
3.1	13–14			13	9–10		3.1
3.2	15	11		14	11	8	3.2
3.3	16	12	10	15	12	9	3.3
3.4	17	13	11				3.4
3.5	18			16			3.5
3.6	19	14	12	17	13	10	3.6
3.7	20	15	13	18	14	11	3.7
3.8	21–22	16	14	19	15–16		3.8
3.9	23	17–18	15	20	17–18	12	3.9
4.0	24	19	16	21	19	13	4.0
4.1	25	20	17	22	20	14–15	4.1
4.2	26	21	18	23	21	16	4.2
4.3	27	22	19	24	22		4.3
4.4	28	23	20	25	23	17	4.4
4.5	29	24	21	26	24	18	4.5
4.6	30	25	22	27		19	4.6
4.7	31	26	23	28	25	20	4.7
4.8	32–33	27		29	26	21	4.8
4.9	34	28–29	24	30	27	22	4.9
5.0	35	30	25	31	28	23–24	5.0
5.1	36	31	26	32–33	29	25–26	5.1
5.2	37–38	32	27	34	30	27	5.2
5.3	39–40	33	28	35	31	28	5.3
5.4		34	29	36		29	5.4
5.5		35–36	30	37	32	30	5.5
5.6		37–38	31	38	33	31–32	5.6
5.7		39–40	32–34	39	34–35	33–34	5.7
5.8			35–37		36	35	5.8
5.9			38–40	40	37	36	5.9
6.0					38	37	6.0
6.1					39	38	6.1
6.2					40	39	6.2
6.3						40	6.3

Predicting future performance with the Hodder Scale

The tests for each term have been designed to provide questions covering a range of demand appropriate to the year and term. In Table 4.7 overleaf you can see at a glance the Hodder Scale score of a pupil in any term, and track to the column to see the anticipated Hodder Scale score they will obtain if they make average progress. As the tests have been designed to challenge pupils around the level at which they are expected to be working, you may find that pupils get similar raw scores from term to term across each year, but their level of performance, as shown in the Hodder Scale score, will of course continue to increase.

You may wish to set targets for the future and monitor progress over a term or year. This is possible for both individual pupils and whole classes, by drawing on the average performance data of over 1,000 pupils in each year group, from term to term and across all the years, in the standardisation sample. Tables 4.7 and 4.8 on page 72 and 74 provide this information.

In Key Stage 2, expected progress is usually about one Hodder Scale Demand (low/mid/high) every term. Some children do better than this, others less well. In Table 4.7 look up the term in which the pupil took the test and follow across to see the anticipated Hodder Scale score they should achieve if they follow the progress of an average pupil.

For example, a pupil who starts Key Stage 2 with a Hodder Scale score of mid 2 on the *PiRA* Year 2 Summer test, and who makes average progress, might be expected to have a Hodder Scale score of 3.0 in the Year 3 Summer test, and 3.8 in the Year 4 Summer test – and ultimately to gain a mid 5 in Year 6 with a *PiRA* prediction of 5.3. In practice, of course, no pupil is 'average' and progress is rarely completely smooth. In addition, the further ahead one is looking, the more tentative are the predictions one can make (see below). The Hodder Scale, however, does provide a well-founded statistical basis for making predictions about performance which can then be modified in the light of actual progress.

Should a pupil do better than anticipated in a subsequent term, move down the row you are reading across to reflect their improved performance. Similarly, if a pupil does not reach the anticipated average score for the next term, then move up to find the Hodder Scale score that they have achieved and read across to see the revised prediction if they now do make average progress.

Monitoring the difference between the *actual* Hodder Scale score and the *predicted* average Hodder Scale score – for an individual pupil or for a whole class – enables you to see if there is increasing divergence or convergence to normal progress.

Table 4.8 on page 74 provides a cross-check opportunity to monitor average progress from the beginning of a year (autumn) to the end of year (summer), in effect skipping the spring data, for Years 3 to 6. This may help provide a snapshot of the likely performance of a pupil or class at the end of a school year. The information in Table 4.8 was obtained via a separate set of equatings to that given in Table 4.7. The results are very similar, but not identical.

Table 4.7: Monitoring and predicting progress on a term-by-term basis
From summer Year 2 through Years 3 and 4

Average Hodder Scale score						
PiRA 2 Summer	*PiRA 3 Autumn*	*PiRA 3 Spring*	*PiRA 3 Summer*	*PiRA 4 Autumn*	*PiRA 4 Spring*	*PiRA 4 Summer*
				1.4	1.7–1.8	2.3
				1.5	1.9	2.3
				1.6	2.0	2.4
			1.7–1.8	1.7–1.9	2.1	2.5–2.6
			1.9	2.0	2.2	2.7
		1.2	2.0	2.1	2.3	2.8
	0.6	1.3–1.4	2.1	2.2	2.4	2.9
0.5	0.6	1.5	2.1	2.2	2.5	3.0
0.6	0.7–0.8	1.6	2.2	2.3	2.5	3.0
0.7	0.8-0.9	1.6	2.2	2.3	2.6	3.1
0.8–0.9	1.0–1.1	1.7	2.2	2.3	2.6	3.1
1.0	1.2	1.8	2.3	2.4	2.7	3.2
1.1	1.3–1.4	1.9	2.4	2.4	2.8	3.2
1.2	1.5–1.6	1.9	2.4	2.5	2.9	3.3
1.3–1.6	1.7–1.8	2.0	2.5	2.5	2.9	3.3
1.7–1.9	1.9	2.0	2.5	2.6	2.9	3.3
2.0	2.0	2.1	2.6	2.7	2.9	3.3
2.0	2.1	2.1	2.6	2.8	3.0	3.4
2.1	2.2	2.1	2.7	2.9	3.1	3.5–3.6
2.3	2.3	2.3	2.8	2.9	3.1	3.5–3.6
2.4	2.4	2.4	2.9	3.0	3.2	3.7
2.5	2.5	2.5	3.0	3.1	3.2	3.8
2.5	2.6	2.6	3.1	3.2	3.3	3.8
2.6	2.7	2.7	3.2	3.3	3.4	3.9
2.6	2.7	2.7	3.2	3.4	3.5–3.6	3.9
2.7	2.8	2.8	3.3	3.5	3.7	4.0
2.8	2.9	2.9	3.4	3.6	3.8	4.1
2.9	3.0	3.0	3.5	3.7	3.8	4.1
3.0	3.0	3.1	3.6	3.8	3.9	4.2
3.0	3.0	3.1	3.6	3.9	3.9	4.2
3.1	3.1	3.2	3.7	4.0	4.0	4.3
3.2	3.2	3.3	3.8	4.1	4.1–4.2	4.4
3.3	3.3	3.4–3.6	3.9	4.2	4.3–4.4	4.5
	3.4–3.5	3.7–3.8	4.0	4.3	4.5–4.6	4.6
	3.6	4.0–4.2	4.1–4.2	4.4–4.5	4.7	4.7
			4.3–4.4	4.6	4.7	4.7
			4.5–4.6	4.7	4.7	4.7
			4.7	4.7	4.8	4.8
				4.8	4.8	4.9
				4.9	4.9	5.0
					5.0	5.1
						5.2

From summer Year 4 through Years 5 and 6

Average Hodder Scale score						
PiRA 4 Summer	PiRA 5 Autumn	PiRA 5 Spring	PiRA 5 Summer	PiRA 6 Autumn	PiRA 6 Spring	PiRA 6 Summer
				2.1	2.3–2.4	3.3
				2.2	2.5–2.6	3.4–3.6
			1.8	2.3	2.7–2.8	3.7–3.8
			1.9	2.4	2.9	3.9
			2.0–2.2	2.5	3.0	3.9
			2.3–2.4	2.6	3.0	3.9
			2.5–2.6	2.7	3.1	4.0
			2.7	2.8	3.2	4.1
		1.8	2.8	2.9	3.3	4.2
		1.9	2.9	3.0–3.1	3.4–3.6	4.3
1.9	2.0	2.0	3.0	3.2	3.7	4.4
2.0	2.1	2.2	3.1	3.3	3.8	4.5
2.1	2.2	2.3	3.2	3.4–3.5	3.8	4.5
2.2	2.4	2.5–2.6	3.3	3.7	3.9	4.7
2.3	2.4	2.7	3.4	3.8–3.9	4.0	4.8
2.4	2.5	2.8	3.5–3.6	4.0	4.0	4.8
2.5–2.6	2.6	2.9	3.7	4.0	4.1	4.9
2.7–2.8	2.7–2.8	2.9	3.8	4.1	4.2	4.9
2.9	2.9	3.0	3.8	4.2	4.3	5.0
3.0	3.0	3.1–3.2	3.9	4.3	4.4	5.0
3.1	3.1	3.3	4.0	4.4	4.5	5.1
3.2	3.2	3.4	4.1	4.5	4.6	5.1
3.3	3.3	3.5–3.6	4.2	4.6	4.7	5.1
3.4	3.4	3.7	4.2	4.7	4.8	5.1
3.5	3.5	3.8	4.2	4.8	4.9	5.2
3.6	3.6	3.9	4.3	4.9	5.0	5.2
3.7	3.7	3.9	4.4	5.0	5.1	5.3
3.8	3.8	4.0	4.5	5.1	5.2	5.3
3.9	3.9	4.1	4.6	5.1	5.3	5.4
4.0	4.0	4.1	4.6	5.2	5.4	5.5
4.1	4.1	4.2	4.7	5.3	5.4	5.5
4.2	4.2	4.3	4.8	5.4	5.5	5.6
4.3	4.3	4.4	4.9	5.5	5.6	5.6
4.4	4.4	4.5	5.0	5.6	5.6	5.6
4.5	4.5	4.6	5.1	5.7	5.7	5.7
4.6	4.6	4.7	5.2	5.7	5.7	5.8
4.7	4.7	4.8	5.2	5.7	5.8	5.8
4.8	4.8	4.8	5.2	5.7	5.8	5.9
4.9	4.9	4.9	5.3	5.8	5.9	6.0
5.0	5.0	5.0	5.4	5.8	5.9	6.0
5.0	5.1	5.1–5.2	5.5	5.8	6.0	6.0
5.1	5.2	5.3	5.6	5.8	6.0	6.1
5.2	5.3	5.4–5.5	5.7	5.8	6.0	6.1
5.3	5.4–5.5	5.6	5.7	5.8	6.1	6.2
	5.6–5.7	5.7	5.8	5.9	6.1	6.2
		5.8–5.9	5.9	5.9	6.2	6.3

Table 4.8: Monitoring and predicting progress from autumn to summer within each Year

Years 3 and 4

Average Hodder Scale score	
PiRA 3 Autumn	PiRA 3 Summer
0.6	2.1
0.7–0.8	2.1
0.9	2.2
1.0–1.1	2.2
1.2	2.2
1.3–1.4	2.3
1.5–1.6	2.4
1.7–1.8	2.5
1.9	2.5
2.0	2.6
2.1	2.6
2.1	2.7
2.2	2.8
2.3	2.9
2.4	3.0
2.5	3.1
2.5	3.2
2.6	3.2
2.6	3.3
2.7	3.3
2.7	3.4
2.8	3.5
2.8	3.6
2.9	3.6
2.9	3.7
2.9	3.8
3.0	3.9
3.0	4.0
3.1	4.1
3.1	4.2
3.2	4.3
3.3	4.4
3.4	4.5
3.5	4.6
3.6	4.7

Average Hodder Scale score	
PiRA 4 Autumn	PiRA 4 Summer
1.6	2.2
1.7–1.9	2.3
2.0	2.4
2.1	2.4
2.2	2.5–2.6
2.2	2.7–2.8
2.3	2.9
2.4	3.0
2.4	3.1
2.5	3.2
2.6	3.2
2.7	3.2
2.8	3.3
2.9	3.4
2.9	3.5
3.0	3.5
3.0	3.6
3.1	3.7
3.2	3.8
3.3	3.8
3.4	3.9
3.5	3.9
3.6	4.0
3.7	4.1
3.8	4.1
3.9	4.2
4.0	4.3
4.1	4.4
4.2	4.4
4.3	4.5
4.4–4.5	4.6
4.6	4.7
4.7	4.7
4.7	4.8
4.8	4.9
4.9	5.0

Years 5 and 6

Average Hodder Scale score	
PiRA 5 Autumn	PiRA 5 Summer
	2.7
2	2.8
2.1	2.9
2.2	3.0
2.3	3.1
2.4	3.2
2.4	3.3
2.5	3.4
2.6	3.5
2.7–2.8	3.6
2.9	3.7
3.0	3.8
3.1	3.9
3.1	4.0
3.2	4.0
3.3	4.1
3.4	4.2
3.5	4.2
3.6	4.2
3.7	4.3
3.8	4.4
3.8	4.5
3.9	4.6
4.0	4.6
4.1	4.7
4.2	4.8
4.3	4.9
4.4	4.9
4.5	5.0
4.6	5.1
4.7	5.2
4.8	5.2
4.9	5.3
5.0	5.4
5.1	5.5
5.2	5.5
5.2	5.6
5.3	5.7–5.8

Average Hodder Scale score	
PiRA 6 Autumn	PiRA 6 Summer
2.0	2.9
2.1	2.9
2.2	3.0–3.2
2.3	3.3
2.4	3.3
2.5	3.4–3.6
2.6	3.7
2.7	3.8
2.7	3.9
2.8	4.0
2.9	4.1
3.0–3.1	4.1
3.2	4.1
3.3	4.2
3.4–3.5	4.3
3.6	4.4
3.7	4.5
3.8–3.9	4.6
4.0	4.7
4.0	4.8
4.1	4.8
4.2	4.9
4.3	5.0
4.4	5.0
4.5	5.0
4.6	5.1
4.7	5.1
4.8	5.2
4.9	5.2
5.0	5.2
5.1	5.3
5.1	5.4
5.2	5.4
5.3	5.5
5.4	5.6
5.5	5.6
5.6	5.7
5.7	5.8–6.0
5.8	6.1
5.9	6.2

The case studies presented in the next section illustrate some of the benefits of mining the *PiRA* data.

Case studies

Case Study 1 – Tarren

Tarren has just started Year 3. He's a summer-born child and had done quite well in Year 1, from the observational measures used to monitor progress. In Year 2 he had been tested using *PiRA* and it showed he was doing well, scoring 18 in the Year 2 Autumn *PiRA*, the equivalent of 2.2 on the Hodder Scale, with a standardised score of 111. However, in the spring term he fell back to a standardised score of 95, scoring only 15 in the Spring *PiRA* test, remaining on the Hodder Scale at 2.2. Although the drop was not significant, it corroborated the class teacher's report that Tarren seemed to be losing confidence.

At the end of the spring term of Year 2, his teacher had looked back at his previous *PiRA* tests and noticed that he was gaining all his marks from the easy questions and seemed to hit a barrier when it came to the harder ones.

Tarren's teacher decided that, for the summer term of Year 2, he would move Tarren to a higher literacy group, in order to give him more experience of answering harder questions in the supportive context of a guided reading group.

The summer term results were much more encouraging (scoring 14 marks, 2.5 on the Hodder Scale and a standardised score of 96). Tarren gained confidence as a reader and was showing progress, albeit his marks showed that he was still below the standardised score of 100 and he still had some catching up to do.

We are so pleased that the issue with his confidence was identified in Year 2. It means that Tarren starts Year 3 in a much stronger position than he was in midway through Year 2, and we also know that we need to keep an eye on his confidence. The fact that we have the background of the *PiRA* tests means that we will notice any future dip quite quickly and will be able to respond swiftly, if necessary.

Case Study 2 – Viktoria

Viktoria started Key Stage 2 working within age-related expectations in some subjects, but her reading and writing did not match her verbal skills. In the summer of Year 3 we assessed her using the Year 2 *PiRA* Summer test again, as she could not cope with the Summer Year 3 *PiRA* test. We found that she had made little or no progress from Key Stage 1 – we actually wondered if she was moving backwards.

In Year 4, we used the Year 2 Autumn and Spring tests, rather than Year 3 or Year 4 *PiRA* tests, to ensure that she could engage with the reading texts and have the questions on the same page as the reading material. These results confirmed her continued lack of progress in Year 4. At a pupil progress interview at the end of the spring term in Year 4, she was identified as a cause for concern.

We undertook an analysis of her three sets of *PiRA* results. The pattern shone out when we marked up her analysis on the record sheet. The bar chart marks showed that she was not gaining any of the inferential marks. That surprised us: although she is an EAL child, she has been in school since the beginning of Year 2 and her spoken English is very colloquial. We knew that her writing level was low – but it always has been and she is a very reluctant writer.

At the pupil progress meeting, we started to think more about the possibility that Viktoria's command of English may not be as good as it seems. Our strategy was to:

- give her additional time with our EAL Teaching Assistant, with the specific intention of looking at idioms and non-literal uses of English;
- use opportunities in ICT to explore her written sentence construction;
- introduce a small-group speaking and listening programme to focus on reasoning and explanations;
- use opportunities in guided reading to explore her use of inference.

The EAL analysis showed that Viktoria did indeed have weaknesses in her understanding of more advanced and subtle English. We were able to target the interventions to address those explicitly. Our anecdotal evidence was that, almost week by week, Viktoria's confidence in answering inferential questions grew. Her access to the rest of the curriculum also improved – as did her willingness to write. We were pleased then, that the summer term *PiRA* results were more encouraging – even though she is still taking tests a year behind where her classmates are and there is obviously still more work to do. The *PiRA* tests were useful in helping us to identify this problem – we should have done so earlier and are reviewing our use of the *PiRA* analyses for all children in all years.

Case Study 3 – Pippa

When Pippa began Year 5 we had high expectations of her – she was predicted to exceed expectations. However, when she sat the *PiRA* Autumn test in October, she scored only 18, only just reaching a standardised score of 90. We were confident that the new *PiRA* tests were sound because other children did as expected. We recognised that we needed to look more carefully at Pippa's reading test.

It wasn't hard to see the problem: Pippa hadn't answered most of the questions. We did an analysis of the questions she had answered and examined the facilities in the mark scheme. This offered us two hypotheses: either she stopped working when she was faced with a harder question, or she was an unusually slow worker. The former seemed less likely, as there was no evidence of her being unwilling to attempt things.

We paid closer attention to Pippa's behaviour during guided reading and noted that she didn't contribute much. Occasionally, she would begin to answer a question, then she would fade out and another child would butt in. This had led the teacher to remember that Pippa had participated, but she hadn't picked up that Pippa didn't actually answer any questions.

When we discussed Pippa with our SENCO, she asked whether the problem was reading comprehension or listening comprehension. That made her teacher look more closely at all of Pippa's learning behaviours and she started to become more concerned. Eventually, Pippa was referred to a speech therapist and the educational psychologist, who recognised that she had significant difficulties in processing language, whether written or spoken.

As she watched Pippa in guided reading, her teacher also recognised that, in addition to reading slowly, Pippa started re-reading the text from the beginning every time a new question was asked. This was a much easier problem to solve and we gave Pippa some highly focused strategies and experience to maximise the efficiency of her reading comprehension and ways to answer tests.

The effectiveness of this strategy was proved in the spring term, even though Pippa was still slow and needed quite a bit more time than others. She scored 26 marks (with a Hodder Scale score of 4.7 and standardised score of 108), which puts her on track to achieve age-related expectations or better if this rate of improvement continues. We have seen a considerable increase in performance because she was given all the time she needed, as we wanted to see what she could do if she had time.

We are very pleased that *PiRA* helped us to identify Pippa's specific difficulty, because it gives us time to work with Pippa to minimise the impact of her difficulties. We also know that we can apply for her to have additional time in her SATs and we have evidence, by giving her enough time in the *PiRA* tests, that the additional time allows her to show what she can do.

Case Study 4 – Max

Our school has always used teacher assessment rather than test information to track pupil progress. We used *PiRA* for the first time two years ago, when we had some new teachers and realised that we needed something to give us external validation of our teacher assessments. The Hodder Scale was particularly helpful, as it enabled us to make links between year-based age-related expectations and former levels.

Max is in Year 6. We worry about him, because his attitude isn't always good and his behaviour can be somewhat challenging. His progress, when measured against previous *PiRA* tests, has been patchy: some terms he made progress, whereas in other terms he appeared to go backwards. This has always puzzled us, because teacher assessment showed a smooth progression. We needed to investigate whether the teacher assessment was optimistic or his engagement with tests was inconsistent.

An analysis of Max's answers in the *PiRA* Year 6 Autumn test gave us some useful feedback about our curriculum and approach:

- A key feature we noticed was that Max gained only one of his marks from the non-fiction text. He had been discreetly observed while doing the test and he seemed just to scan the non-fiction material rather than read it, even though there was no time pressure on him. We realised that we had been focusing almost exclusively on fiction in our teaching over the term. Luckily, the fact that *PiRA* tests explore a wide range of texts alerted us to this difficulty.

- Max made a lot of careless mistakes. He tends to do this in class too but, when we ask him to think more carefully, he can often give good answers. Of course, in a test situation there is no feedback.

- Our observation seemed to indicate that he appeared to lose confidence immediately he found a question he couldn't do, and this meant that he scored badly from that point on until he started the next text.

This analysis helped us understand that the tests were consistent and the teacher's assessment was accurate. However, it also made us reassess the breadth of texts our children were reading and the way in which we prepare children to take tests. Children need to think carefully without our scaffolding feedback and they need to understand that easier questions can follow harder ones. We shall spend some time getting children to adopt better coping strategies under test conditions.

The SENCO tried Max out with some coloured reading rulers to see whether scotopic sensitivity might account for the inconsistencies in his test results. He discovered that a very deep rose colour made the 'paper behind the writing stop moving around'. Since Max has been using this reading ruler, he has made fewer careless mistakes and seems to be more confident at trying more challenging questions.

We had discussed whether we would still be able to use the data we gained from the first edition of *PiRA* with the new tests, but it turned out that it was no problem. The anchor for us was the Hodder Scale, which didn't move. We are pleased that the new tests are more challenging, because that will push our children and make us raise our game too.

Standardisation sample

Overall, 46 schools took part in the original standardisation of the *PiRA* tests. The government school performance website showed that, in the Key Stage 2 national tests for 2008, those schools participating in the standardisation had 80.9 per cent of their pupils gaining a level 4 or above (of whom 28.5 per cent gained a level 5).

The government statistics showed that, in 2008, 81 per cent of pupils nationally achieved level 4 or above, and in 2009, 79 per cent achieved level 4 or above. Overall, therefore, the *PiRA* schools' performance was very closely representative of primary schools across the country. The schools also reflected a wide cross-section in terms of school size and location and the language mix of the pupils, as shown in Tables 5.1 and 5.2.

Table 5.1: Description of schools in the original standardisation, including home languages of pupils

Language mix of pupils	Demography of school			
	Central large town/city	Suburban large town/city	Small town	Village
English as only home language	–	2	3	5
Fewer than 5 different home languages	2	5	3	10
Between 6–9 different home languages	3	6	1	–
More than 20 home languages	3	3	–	–
Total	8	16	7	15

In total, 10,846 pupils took part in the original standardisation although, through absence when tests were taken and as a result of moving schools and so on, the core cohort that provided the 'all-through' term-on-term links was between 7,500 and 8,000 pupils – that is, over 1,000 per year group, except in the Reception year where it was 850. (A number of Early Years teachers did not wish to use a formal test with the very youngest children.) Table 5.3 on page 82 provides reliability information about the standardisation sample.

Table 5.2: Information about the sample used in the equating study (close to 5,000 pupils took part in the equating study from each term 32 schools widely distributed across England)

Language mix of pupils	Demography of school			
	Central large town/city	Suburban large town/city	Small town	Village
English as only home language	1	–	1	2
Fewer than 5 different home languages	–	4	6	9
Between 6–19 different home languages	1	5	–	–
More than 20 different home languages	1	2	–	–
Total	3	11	7	11

Reliability

The *reliability* of a test indicates whether or not we would get similar results from repeated administrations of the test with similar samples of pupils. An appropriate measure of test reliability for *PiRA* is Cronbach's alpha (α), which measures internal consistency reliability. A value above 0.60 is considered the minimum acceptable for most forms of educational assessment. This information for each test is given in Table 5.3 overleaf and shows that the tests are extremely reliable.

Test theory tells us that test reliability is also related to test length and suggests that any test should comprise 25 or more marks to achieve reasonable reliability.

For tests targeting a particular age range, we use a standardisation method based on *percentile norms* – the fundamental principle being that scores at the same percentile rank are comparable. Hence a pupil at, say, the 30th percentile in his/her age group has the same relative ability as a pupil at the 30th percentile in any other age group. The standardisation procedure that we have used for these tests is called the *non-parallel linear regression model*. It is the recognised method for age standardising educational tests.

Any scores derived from a short test are subject to some margin of error. This does not mean that a child has been assessed incorrectly, but rather that we are making a statistical estimate of the accuracy of the test as a measuring instrument. There are two ways of reporting the margin of error. One is the standard error of measurement ('SE measurement' in Table 5.3 overleaf), the other is the 90 per cent confidence band.

The 90 per cent confidence bands are calculated during the fitting of linear regression lines to the P5, P10 ... P90, P95 isopercentiles during the age standardisation process. The confidence bands are not the same measure as the standard error of measurement shown in the item analysis report which is calculated directly from pupils' raw test data.

The 90 per cent confidence band for Key Stage 2 *PiRA* age-standardised scores is +/– 4. This means, for example, that for a child aged 9:2 (nine years and two months) who obtains a raw score of 15 marks on the Autumn Year 4 test and hence a standardised score of 98, we can say with 90 per cent confidence that their 'true' standardised score lies between 94 and 102. Table 5.3 overleaf gives the reliability data for each test.

In Table 5.3, the 'Pearson coefficient' is a measure of the correlation between pupils' *PiRA* raw scores and either their national test scores or their teacher-assessed levels as supplied by schools. A perfect match would be 1. The fact that these are higher in the summer term reflects the fact that this is when results are 'officially' reported, as well as the teachers' longer familiarity with their pupils and their individual attainment.

Table 5.3: Sample statistics and reliability measures

PiRA 3

	1st edition standardisation		
	PiRA 3 Autumn (2009)	PiRA 3 Spring (2010)	PiRA 3 Summer (2010)
Sample size	1,215	1,205	1,122
Boys	612	590	559
Girls	603	615	563
Mean	22.6	21.3	22.6
SE measurement	2.48	2.50	2.56
Cronbach alpha	0.94	0.93	0.91
Pearson coefficient	0.78	0.77	0.79
90% confidence limit	+/−3.97	+/−4.00	+/−4.10
95% confidence limit	+/−4.96	+/−5.00	+/−5.12
	2nd edition equating study (2015)		
	PiRA 3 Autumn	PiRA 3 Spring	PiRA 3 Summer
Sample size	817	1,023	805
Mean	22.7	23.1	22.1

PiRA 4

	1st edition standardisation		
	PiRA 4 Autumn (2009)	PiRA 4 Spring (2010)	PiRA 4 Summer (2010)
Sample size	1,251	1,249	1,120
Boys	653	655	583
Girls	598	594	537
Mean	18.0	21.3	21.6
SE measurement	2.62	2.60	2.26
Cronbach alpha	0.92	0.93	0.92
Pearson coefficient	0.74	0.77	0.78
90% confidence limit	+/−4.19	+/−4.16	+/−3.62
95% confidence limit	+/−5.24	+/−5.20	+/−4.52
	2nd edition equating study (2015)		
	PiRA 4 Autumn	PiRA 4 Spring	PiRA 4 Summer
Sample size	937	903	782
Mean	18.2	23.9	22.6

PiRA 5

	1st edition standardisation		
	PiRA 5 Autumn (2009)	PiRA 5 Spring (2010)	PiRA 5 Summer (2010)
Sample size	1,197	1,158	1,056
Boys	586	569	516
Girls	611	589	540
Mean	19.9	18.9	21.5
SE measurement	2.73	2.60	2.63
Cronbach alpha	0.91	0.93	0.90
Pearson coefficient	0.76	0.76	0.78
90% confidence limit	+/−4.37	+/−4.16	+/−4.21
95% confidence limit	+/−5.46	+/−4.20	+/−5.26
	2nd edition equating study (2015)		
	PiRA 5 Autumn	PiRA 5 Spring (2015)	PiRA 5 Summer
Sample size	920	881	704
Mean	21.3	21.4	19.4

PiRA 6

	1st edition standardisation			
	PiRA 6 Autumn (2009)	PiRA 6 Spring (2010)	PiRA 6 Summer (2010)	PiRA 6 Summer (2009)
Sample size	1,255	1,217	1,109	731
Boys	633	607	553	362
Girls	622	610	556	369
Mean	23.5	23.0	22.2	22.9
SE measurement	2.68	2.59	2.64	2.64
Cronbach alpha	0.89	0.92	0.91	0.89
Pearson coefficient	0.77	0.74	0.64	0.72
90% confidence limit	+/−4.29	+/−4.14	+/−4.22	+/−4.22
90% confidence limit	+/−5.36	+/−5.18	+/−5.28	+/−5.28
	2nd edition equating study (2015)			
	PiRA 6 Autumn	PiRA 6 Spring	PiRA 6 Summer	
Sample size	768	801	704	
Mean	23.3	21.2	21.4	

The range of the Pearson coefficients from the equating studies was between 0.94 and 0.99 across the eight tests, which indicates the two tests – original and new – were incredibly closely aligned, and the equating may be completely trusted.

Gender differences

In all years and terms, girls out-perform boys. This is consistent with national patterns of reading tests and English tests in general.

Table 5.4: Average marks (raw scores) for the 1st edition PiRA tests, showing gender differences

PiRA Autumn 1st edition	PiRA 3	PiRA 4	PiRA 5	PiRA 6
Mean score	22.6	18.0	19.9	23.5
Avg boys	20.8	17.0	19.2	23.0
Avg girls	24.4	19.4	20.4	24.2
Max. score	40	40	40	40

PiRA Spring 1st edition	PiRA 3	PiRA 4	PiRA 5	PiRA 6
Mean score	21.3	21.3	18.9	23.0
Avg boys	19.8	20.2	17.8	21.9
Avg girls	22.8	22.5	20.0	24.1
Max. score	40	40	40	40

PiRA Summer 1st edition	PiRA 3	PiRA 4	PiRA 5	PiRA 6
Mean score	22.6	21.6	21.5	22.2
Avg boys	21.3	20.7	20.3	21.4
Avg girls	24.0	22.6	22.6	23.5
Max. score	40	40	40	40

Validity

Strong *face validity* for a test like *PiRA* means that the test addresses the material in the curriculum which the children have studied and been taught. Each test in the original *PiRA* series, from Reception to Year 6, was written to follow the national guidelines for the second half of the previous term and the first half of the term the test is set for. This ensured that these tests, which should ideally be taken soon after half-term each term, meet the *validity* criterion. The revision process used the information in the 2014 National Curriculum and the 2015 test frameworks to confirm that each question from the first edition that remained was valid and that new questions replaced those that did not match the new curriculum and assessment requirements.

The *validity* of the age standardisation is improved if there is good correlation between pupils' test scores and age. Additionally, the test itself must have high reliability (see above) so that the results would be replicated by repeated administrations of the test. Children who were in Year 2 and Year 6 who took the same Summer *PiRA* tests in subsequent years of the original standardisation showed very similar performance.

To ensure validity, we also compared the original *PiRA* tests with the Optional Tests for Years 3, 4 and 5, and the 2009 Key Stage 1 and Key Stage 2 national tests, applying the same standards criteria to confirm that *PiRA* tests were of similar demand in terms of coverage of sublevels. While the *PiRA* tests contain less text material, there is less referencing to specific individual paragraphs and more emphasis on reading for meaning, as recommended in *Letters and Sounds* once phonics have been established. In general, performance on *PiRA* has increased as illustrated when the means from 2009/10 and 2015 are compared for the original tests. These are provided for each test at the end of the appropriate mark scheme.

Table 5.5: *PiRA* tests analysed for range of demand

	P scales			Hodder Scale of Demand																Total
	P6	P7	P8	low 1	mid 1	high 1	low 2	mid 2	high 2	low 3	mid 3	high 3	low 4	mid 4	high 4	low 5	mid 5	high 5	6	
PiRA R Spring	5	4	9	5	2															25
PiRA R Summer	3	3	5	6	7	1														25
PiRA 1 Autumn				11	9	3	2													25
PiRA 1 Spring				10	6	4	3	2												25
PiRA 1 Summer				4	5	9	4	3												25
PiRA 2 Autumn				5	1	10	3	4	2											25
PiRA 2 Spring				2	2	4	8	6	1	1	0	1								25
PiRA 2 Summer					1	1	3	6	5	4	3	2								25
PiRA 3 Autumn				2	2	0	10	8	2	11	5									40
PiRA 3 Spring					2	3	1	4	7	7	9	3	4							40
PiRA 3 Summer						1	2	2	6	9	9	6	5							40
PiRA 4 Autumn						1	0	8	6	4	4	6	7	4						40
PiRA 4 Spring							1	5	3	11	4	6	4	4	2					40
PiRA 4 Summer							1	2	6	4	8	9	4	2	4	1				40
PiRA 5 Autumn									4	4	12	4	8	3	1	2	1	1		40
PiRA 5 Spring									2	2	6	5	8	6	5	5	1			40
PiRA 5 Summer										3	3	3	5	13	8	4	1			40
PiRA 6 Autumn										6	3	6	5	9	7	3	1			40
PiRA 6 Spring											4	2	9	11	5	4	3	0	2	40
PiRA 6 Summer											4	4	4	9	6	6	3	2	2	40
	P6	P7	P8	low 1	mid 1	high 1	low 2	mid 2	high 2	low 3	mid 3	high 3	low 4	mid 4	high 4	low 5	mid 5	high 5	6	

Standardised scores

Note: There is no formal definition as to which standardised score is the threshold for a child to be at the expected stage (either for part way through the year or at the end of the year).

A standardised score of 100 is the norm (mean) for the cohort and it is anticipated that this will be at the expected stage for that term. Most teachers and schools are comfortable that a standardised score of 95 can also be the threshold for the expected stage, while the consensus seems to be that around 90 is the lowest acceptable score that indicates expected progress. However, schools will need to use all the evidence available to make this judgement.

PiRA 3 Autumn

Hodder Scale	Raw score	Standardised score
1.1	1	67
1.2	2	69
1.4	3	70
1.6	4	72
1.8	5	74
1.9	6	75
2.0	7	77
2.1	8	78
2.1	9	80
2.2	10	82
2.2	11	83
2.3	12	85
2.3	13	86
2.4	14	88
2.4	15	89
2.5	16	91
2.5	17	93
2.5	18	94
2.6	19	96
2.6	20	97
2.7	21	99
2.7	22	101
2.8	23	102
2.8	24	104
2.8	25	105
2.9	26	107
2.9	27	109
3.0	28	110
3.0	29	112
3.1	30	113
3.1	31	115
3.2	32	117
3.3	33	118
3.4	34	120
3.5	35	121
3.6	36	123
3.7	37	125
3.8	38	126
3.9	39	128
4.0	40	130

PiRA 3 Spring

Hodder Scale	Raw score	Standardised score
<1.4	1	59
<1.4	2	61
1.4	3	63
1.5	4	65
1.6	5	67
1.7	6	69
1.8	7	70
1.9	8	72
2.0	9	74
2.0	10	76
2.1	11	78
2.1	12	80
2.1	13	82
2.2	14	83
2.2	15	85
2.3	16	87
2.4	17	89
2.5	18	91
2.6	19	93
2.6	20	95
2.7	21	96
2.8	22	98
2.8	23	100
2.9	24	102
2.9	25	104
3.0	26	106
3.1	27	108
3.2	28	109
3.4	29	111
3.6	30	113
3.7	31	115
3.8	32	117
3.9	33	119
4.0	34	121
4.1	35	122
4.1	36	124
4.2	37	126
4.2	38	128
4.3	39	130
4.3	40	132

PiRA 3 Summer

Hodder Scale	Raw score	Standardised score
1.4	1	55
1.5	2	57
1.6	3	59
1.7	4	61
1.8	5	63
1.9	6	65
2.0	7	68
2.1	8	70
2.2	9	72
2.2	10	74
2.3	11	76
2.4	12	78
2.5	13	80
2.6	14	83
2.6	15	85
2.7	16	87
2.8	17	89
2.9	18	91
2.9	19	93
3.0	20	96
3.1	21	98
3.2	22	100
3.2	23	102
3.3	24	104
3.4	25	106
3.5	26	108
3.6	27	111
3.7	28	113
3.8	29	115
3.9	30	117
4.0	31	119
4.3	32	121
4.4	33	124
4.5	34	126
4.6	35	128
4.7	36	130
4.8	>36	134

PiRA 4 Autumn

Hodder Scale	Raw score	Standardised score
1.6	1	68
1.9	2	70
2.0	3	72
2.1	4	74
2.2	5	75
2.2	6	77
2.3	7	79
2.4	8	80
2.4	9	83
2.5	10	84
2.6	11	86
2.7	12	88
2.8	13	90
2.9	14	92
3.0	15	93
3.0	16	95
3.1	17	97
3.2	18	99
3.3	19	101
3.5	20	102
3.6	21	104
3.7	22	106
3.8	23	108
3.9	24	110
4.0	25	111
4.1	26	113
4.3	27	115
4.5	28	117
4.6	29	118
4.7	30	120
4.7	31	122
4.8	32	124
4.8	33	126
4.9	34	127
4.9	35	129
5.0	36–40	131

PiRA 4 Spring

Hodder Scale	Raw score	Standardised score
<1.9	1	58
<1.9	2	60
<1.9	3	62
<1.9	4	64
<1.9	5	66
1.9	6	67
2.0	7	69
2.1	8	71
2.2	9	73
2.3	10	75
2.4	11	77
2.5	12	78
2.6	13	80
2.7	14	82
2.8	15	84
2.9	16	86
2.9	17	88
3.0	18	89
3.1	19	91
3.1	20	93
3.2	21	95
3.3	22	97
3.4	23	99
3.6	24	100
3.7	25	102
3.8	26	104
3.9	27	106
3.9	28	108
4.0	29	110
4.2	30	111
4.5	31	113
4.6	32	115
4.7	33	117
4.7	34	119
4.8	35	121
4.8	36	122
4.9	37	124
4.9	38	126
5.0	39	128
5.0	40	130

PiRA 4 Summer

Hodder Scale	Raw score	Standardised score
1.7	1	58
1.8	2	64
1.9	3	65
2.0	4	67
2.1	5	69
2.2	6	71
2.2	7	72
2.3	8	74
2.4	9	76
2.6	10	78
2.8	11	79
2.9	12	81
3.0	13	83
3.1	14	85
3.2	15	87
3.2	16	88
3.3	17	90
3.4	18	92
3.5	19	94
3.6	20	95
3.7	21	97
3.8	22	99
3.9	23	101
4.0	24	103
4.1	25	104
4.2	26	106
4.3	27	108
4.4	28	110
4.5	29	111
4.6	30	113
4.7	31	115
4.8	32	117
4.9	33	119
4.9	34	120
5.0	35	122
5.0	36	124
5.1	37	126
5.1	38	127
5.2	39–40	131

PiRA 5 Autumn

Hodder Scale	Raw score	Standardised score
1.9	1	57
2.0	2	59
2.1	3	61
2.2	4	63
2.3	5	65
2.4	6	67
2.4	7	69
2.5	8	71
2.6	9	73
2.8	10	75
2.9	11	77
3.0	12	79
3.1	13	80
3.1	14	82
3.2	15	84
3.3	16	86
3.4	17	88
3.5	18	90
3.6	19	92
3.7	20	94
3.8	21	96
3.8	22	98
3.9	23	100
4.0	24	101
4.1	25	103
4.2	26	105
4.3	27	107
4.4	28	109
4.5	29	111
4.6	30	113
4.7	31	115
4.8	32	117
4.8	33	119
4.9	34	121
5.0	35	123
5.1	36	124
5.2	37	126
5.2	38	128
5.3	39	130
5.3	40	132

PiRA 5 Spring

Hodder Scale	Raw score	Standardised score
	1	64
<1.9	2	65
	3	67
1.9	4	69
2.2	5	71
2.6	6	72
2.8	7	74
2.9	8	76
2.9	9	78
3.0	10	80
3.2	11	81
3.3	12	83
3.4	13	85
3.6	14	87
3.7	15	88
3.8	16	90
3.9	17	92
3.9	18	94
4.0	19	96
4.1	20	97
4.2	21	99
4.3	22	101
4.4	23	103
4.5	24	105
4.6	25	106
4.7	26	108
4.8	27	110
4.9	28	112
4.9	29	113
5.0	30	115
5.1	31	117
5.2	32	119
5.3	33	121
5.4	34	122
5.5	35	124
5.5	36	126
5.6	37	128
5.6	38	129
5.7	39	131
5.7	40	133

PiRA 5 Summer

Hodder Scale	Raw score	Standardised score
1.8	1	62
1.9	2	64
2.0	3	66
2.4	4	68
2.6	5	71
2.7	6	73
2.8	7	75
2.9	8	77
3.0	9	79
3.3	10	81
3.4	11	83
3.6	12	85
3.7	13	87
3.8	14	89
3.9	15	91
4.0	16	93
4.1	17	95
4.2	18	97
4.3	19	99
4.4	20	101
4.5	21	103
4.6	22	105
4.7	23	107
4.9	24	109
5.0	25	111
5.1	26	113
5.2	27	115
5.3	28	118
5.4	29	120
5.5	30	122
5.6	31	124
5.7	32	126
5.7	33	128
5.7	34	130
5.8	35–37	133
5.9	38–40	134

PiRA 6 Autumn

Hodder Scale	Raw score	Standardised score
1.9	1	60
2.0	2	61
2.1	3	63
2.2	4	65
2.3	5	67
2.4	6	68
2.5	7	70
2.6	8	72
2.7	9	74
2.7	10	75
2.8	11	77
2.9	12	79
3.1	13	81
3.2	14	82
3.3	15	84
3.5	16	86
3.6	17	88
3.7	18	89
3.8	19	91
3.9	20	93
4.0	21	94
4.1	22	96
4.2	23	98
4.3	24	100
4.4	25	101
4.5	26	103
4.6	27	105
4.7	28	107
4.8	29	108
4.9	30	110
5.0	31	112
5.1	32	114
5.1	33	115
5.2	34	117
5.3	35	119
5.4	36	121
5.5	37	122
5.6	38	124
5.7	39	126
5.9	40	128

PiRA 6 Spring

Hodder Scale	Raw score	Standardised score
	1	63
<2.4	2	65
	3	66
2.4	4	68
2.6	5	70
2.8	6	72
2.9	7	74
3.0	8	75
3.1	9	77
3.1	10	79
3.2	11	81
3.3	12	83
3.6	13	84
3.7	14	86
3.8	15	88
3.8	16	90
3.9	17	92
3.9	18	93
4.0	19	95
4.1	20	97
4.2	21	99
4.3	22	101
4.4	23	102
4.5	24	104
4.7	25	106
4.8	26	108
4.9	27	110
5.0	28	111
5.1	29	113
5.2	30	115
5.3	31	117
5.5	32	119
5.6	33	120
5.7	34	122
5.7	35	124
5.8	36	126
5.9	37	128
6.0	38	130
6.1	39	131
6.2	40	133

PiRA 6 Summer

Hodder Scale	Raw score	Standardised score
2.1	1	60
2.2	2	62
2.3	3	64
2.6	4	66
2.7	5	68
2.8	6	70
2.9	7	72
3.2	8	74
3.3	9	76
3.6	10	78
3.7	11	80
3.9	12	82
4.0	13	83
4.1	14	85
4.1	15	87
4.2	16	89
4.4	17	91
4.5	18	93
4.6	19	95
4.7	20	97
4.8	21	99
4.9	22	101
5.0	23	103
5.0	24	105
5.1	25	107
5.1	26	109
5.2	27	111
5.3	28	113
5.4	29	115
5.5	30	117
5.6	31	119
5.6	32	121
5.7	33	123
5.7	34	125
5.8	35	127
5.9	36	129
6.0	37	130
6.1	38	131
6.2	39	132
6.3	40	133

Age-standardised scores

PiRA 3 Autumn

Raw score	Age in years and completed months																Raw score
	6:5	6:6	6:7	6:8	6:9	6:10	6:11	7:0	7:1	7:2	7:3	7:4	7:5	7:6	7:7	7:8	
1	87	86	86	85	85	84	84	83	83	82	82	81	81	81	80	80	1
2	88	87	87	86	86	85	85	85	84	84	83	83	82	82	82	81	2
3	89	88	88	87	87	87	86	86	85	85	85	84	84	83	83	82	3
4	90	90	89	89	88	88	87	87	86	86	86	85	85	85	84	84	4
5	91	91	90	90	89	89	88	88	87	87	87	86	86	85	85	85	5
6	93	92	92	91	90	90	89	89	88	88	87	87	87	86	86	86	6
7	94	93	93	92	92	91	91	90	90	89	89	88	88	87	87	87	7
8	94	94	94	93	93	92	92	91	91	90	90	89	89	88	88	87	8
9	95	95	95	94	94	93	93	92	92	91	91	90	90	89	89	88	9
10	96	96	95	95	95	94	94	93	93	93	92	92	91	91	90	90	10
11	97	97	96	96	96	95	95	94	94	93	93	93	92	92	91	91	11
12	98	97	97	97	96	96	96	95	95	94	94	94	93	93	92	92	12
13	99	98	98	97	97	97	96	96	96	95	95	95	94	94	93	93	13
14	100	99	99	98	98	98	97	97	97	96	96	95	95	95	94	94	14
15	101	100	100	99	99	99	98	98	97	97	97	96	96	96	95	95	15
16	102	101	101	101	100	100	99	99	98	98	98	97	97	96	96	96	16
17	103	103	102	102	101	101	100	100	99	99	99	99	99	98	97	97	17
18	104	104	103	103	102	102	102	101	101	100	100	99	99	98	98	97	18
19	106	105	105	104	104	103	103	102	102	101	101	100	100	99	99	98	19
20	107	107	106	106	105	105	104	104	103	103	102	102	101	101	100	100	20
21	108	108	107	107	107	106	106	105	105	104	104	103	103	102	102	101	21
22	109	109	109	108	108	108	107	107	106	106	105	105	104	104	103	102	22
23	111	111	110	110	109	109	109	108	108	107	107	106	106	106	105	104	23
24	113	113	112	112	111	111	110	110	109	109	108	108	107	107	107	106	24
25	115	114	114	114	113	113	112	112	111	111	110	110	109	109	108	108	25
26	116	116	115	115	115	115	114	114	114	113	113	112	112	111	110	110	26
27	118	118	118	117	117	117	116	116	115	115	115	114	114	113	113	112	27
28	120	120	120	120	119	119	119	118	118	117	117	117	116	115	115	115	28
29	122	122	122	122	122	121	121	121	121	120	120	119	119	119	118	118	29
30	125	124	124	124	124	124	123	123	123	123	123	122	122	122	121	121	30
31	127	127	127	127	127	127	126	126	126	126	126	125	125	125	124	124	31
32	130	130	130	130	130	130	130	130	130	130	130	129	129	129	129	129	32
33																	33
34–40				Award >130 for all scores in this area												34–40
	6:5	6:6	6:7	6:8	6:9	6:10	6:11	7:0	7:1	7:2	7:3	7:4	7:5	7:6	7:7	7:8	

Raw score	Age in years and completed months																Raw score
	7:9	7:10	7:11	8:0	8:1	8:2	8:3	8:4	8:5	8:6	8:7	8:8	8:9	8:10	8:11	9:0	
1	79	79	78	78	78	77	77	77	76	76	76	76	75	75	74	74	1
2	81	80	80	79	79	79	78	78	78	77	77	77	77	76	76	76	2
3	82	82	81	81	81	80	80	79	79	79	78	78	78	78	77	77	3
4	83	83	82	82	82	81	81	81	80	80	80	79	79	79	78	78	4
5	84	84	84	83	83	82	82	82	81	81	81	81	80	80	80	79	5
6	85	85	85	84	84	84	83	83	83	82	82	82	81	81	81	80	6
7	86	86	86	85	85	85	84	84	84	83	83	83	82	82	82	81	7
8	87	87	86	86	86	85	85	85	85	84	84	84	83	83	83	82	8
9	88	88	87	87	87	86	86	86	85	85	85	84	84	84	83	83	9
10	89	89	88	88	87	87	87	86	86	86	85	85	85	85	84	84	10
11	90	90	89	89	88	88	87	87	87	86	86	86	86	85	85	85	11
12	91	91	90	90	89	89	88	88	88	87	87	87	86	86	86	86	12
13	92	92	91	91	90	90	89	89	89	88	88	87	87	87	86	86	13
14	93	93	92	92	92	91	91	90	90	89	89	88	88	88	87	87	14
15	94	94	93	93	93	92	92	91	91	90	90	89	89	88	88	88	15
16	95	95	94	94	94	93	93	92	92	91	91	90	90	89	89	89	16
17	96	96	95	95	94	94	94	93	93	92	92	91	91	90	90	90	17
18	97	97	96	96	95	95	95	94	94	93	93	92	92	91	91	91	18
19	98	98	97	97	96	96	96	95	95	94	94	93	93	93	92	92	19
20	99	99	98	98	97	97	97	96	96	95	95	94	94	93	93	93	20
21	101	100	99	99	98	98	97	97	97	96	96	95	95	94	94	94	21
22	102	101	101	100	100	99	99	98	98	97	97	96	96	95	95	95	22
23	104	103	102	102	101	101	100	99	99	98	98	97	97	96	96	96	23
24	106	105	104	103	103	102	102	101	100	100	99	99	98	98	97	97	24
25	107	107	106	106	105	104	103	103	102	101	101	100	99	99	98	98	25
26	109	109	108	107	107	106	106	105	104	103	103	102	101	101	100	99	26
27	112	111	110	110	109	108	108	107	106	106	105	104	103	102	102	101	27
28	114	114	113	113	112	111	110	109	109	108	107	107	106	105	104	103	28
29	117	116	116	115	115	114	114	113	112	111	110	109	108	108	107	106	29
30	121	120	120	119	119	118	117	116	116	115	114	113	113	111	110	109	30
31	124	124	123	123	123	122	122	121	121	120	119	118	117	116	115	114	31
32	129	129	128	128	128	128	127	127	126	126	125	125	124	124	123	122	32
33															130	129	33
34–40					Award >130 for all scores in this area												34–40
	7:9	7:10	7:11	8:0	8:1	8:2	8:3	8:4	8:5	8:6	8:7	8:8	8:9	8:10	8:11	9:0	

PiRA 3 Spring

Raw score	\multicolumn{13}{c}{Age in years and completed months}												Raw score
	7:0	7:1	7:2	7:3	7:4	7:5	7:6	7:7	7:8	7:9	7:10	7:11	8:0	
1	78	78	77	77	76	76	75	74	74	73	73	72	72	1
2	80	79	79	78	78	77	77	76	76	75	75	74	74	2
3	82	81	81	80	80	79	78	78	77	77	76	76	76	3
4	83	83	82	82	81	81	80	80	79	79	78	78	77	4
5	85	84	84	83	83	82	82	81	81	80	80	79	79	5
6	86	86	85	85	84	84	83	83	82	82	81	81	80	6
7	88	87	87	86	86	85	85	84	84	83	83	82	82	7
8	89	88	88	88	87	87	86	86	85	85	84	84	83	8
9	90	90	89	89	88	88	87	87	86	86	85	85	84	9
10	91	91	90	90	90	89	89	88	88	87	87	86	86	10
11	92	92	91	91	91	90	90	89	89	89	88	88	87	11
12	93	93	92	92	91	91	91	90	90	90	89	89	88	12
13	95	94	94	93	93	92	92	91	91	91	90	90	90	13
14	96	96	95	95	94	94	93	92	92	92	91	91	91	14
15	98	97	97	96	96	95	95	94	93	93	92	92	91	15
16	99	99	98	98	97	97	96	95	95	94	94	93	93	16
17	100	100	99	99	99	98	98	97	96	96	95	95	94	17
18	102	101	101	100	100	99	99	98	98	97	97	96	96	18
19	103	103	102	102	101	101	100	100	99	99	98	98	97	19
20	105	105	104	103	103	102	101	101	100	100	99	99	99	20
21	107	106	106	105	104	104	103	102	102	101	101	100	100	21
22	109	108	107	107	106	106	105	104	104	103	102	102	101	22
23	110	110	109	109	108	107	107	106	106	105	104	104	103	23
24	112	112	111	110	110	109	109	108	107	107	106	105	105	24
25	114	113	113	112	112	111	110	110	109	109	108	107	107	25
26	116	116	115	114	114	113	112	112	111	111	110	109	109	26
27	118	118	117	116	116	115	115	114	113	112	112	111	111	27
28	120	120	119	119	118	117	117	116	115	115	114	113	113	28
29	123	122	122	121	120	120	119	118	118	117	116	116	115	29
30	126	125	124	124	123	122	122	121	120	119	119	118	117	30
31	130	129	128	127	126	125	124	124	123	122	121	121	120	31
32					130	129	128	127	126	125	124	124	123	32
33									130	129	128	127	126	33
34														34
35														35
36			Award >130 for all scores in this area											36
37														37
38–40														38–40
	7:0	7:1	7:2	7:3	7:4	7:5	7:6	7:7	7:8	7:9	7:10	7:11	8:0	

Raw score	8:1	8:2	8:3	8:4	8:5	8:6	8:7	8:8	8:9	8:10	8:11	9:0	9:1	Raw score
					Age in years and completed months									
1	71	71	70	70				Award <70 for all scores in this area						1
2	73	73	72	72	71	71	70	70						2
3	75	75	74	73	73	72	72	71	71	71	70	70		3
4	77	76	76	75	75	74	74	73	73	72	72	71	71	4
5	78	78	77	77	76	76	76	75	75	74	74	73	73	5
6	80	79	79	78	78	77	77	77	76	76	75	75	74	6
7	81	81	80	80	79	79	78	78	78	77	77	76	76	7
8	83	82	82	81	81	80	80	79	79	79	78	78	77	8
9	84	84	83	83	82	82	81	81	80	80	80	79	79	9
10	85	85	84	84	83	83	83	82	82	81	81	81	80	10
11	87	86	86	85	85	84	84	83	83	83	82	82	81	11
12	88	88	87	87	86	86	85	85	84	84	83	83	83	12
13	89	89	88	88	87	87	87	86	86	85	85	84	84	13
14	90	90	89	89	89	88	88	87	87	86	86	85	85	14
15	91	91	90	90	90	89	89	89	88	88	87	87	86	15
16	92	92	91	91	91	90	90	90	89	89	88	88	88	16
17	94	93	92	92	92	91	91	91	90	90	90	89	89	17
18	95	95	94	93	93	92	92	91	91	91	90	90	90	18
19	97	96	95	95	94	94	93	92	92	92	91	91	91	19
20	98	98	97	96	96	95	95	94	94	93	92	92	92	20
21	99	99	98	98	97	97	96	96	95	95	94	93	93	21
22	101	100	100	99	99	98	98	97	97	96	95	95	94	22
23	102	102	101	101	100	100	99	99	98	98	97	96	96	23
24	104	103	103	102	101	101	100	100	99	99	98	98	97	24
25	106	105	105	104	103	103	102	101	101	100	100	99	99	25
26	108	107	107	106	105	105	104	103	102	102	101	101	100	26
27	110	109	109	108	107	107	106	105	105	104	103	102	102	27
28	112	111	111	110	109	109	108	107	107	106	105	104	104	28
29	114	113	113	112	111	111	110	109	109	108	107	107	106	29
30	117	116	115	114	114	113	112	112	111	110	109	109	108	30
31	119	118	118	117	116	116	115	114	113	112	112	111	110	31
32	122	121	120	120	119	118	117	117	116	115	114	113	112	32
33	125	124	124	123	122	121	120	119	118	118	117	116	115	33
34	130	129	128	127	126	124	124	123	122	121	120	119	118	34
35					130	129	128	127	126	124	124	123	122	35
36										130	128	127	126	36
37														37
38–40			Award >130 for all scores in this area											38–40
	8:1	8:2	8:3	8:4	8:5	8:6	8:7	8:8	8:9	8:10	8:11	9:0	9:1	

PiRA 3 Summer

Raw score	\multicolumn{13}{c}{Age in years and completed months}												Raw score
	7:3	7:4	7:5	7:6	7:7	7:8	7:9	7:10	7:11	8:0	8:1	8:2	8:3	
1	70	70	70	\multicolumn{9}{c}{Award <70 for all scores in this area}									1
2	71	71	71	71	71	71	70	70	70	70	70	70		2
3	73	73	72	72	72	72	72	72	72	72	72	71	71	3
4	74	74	74	74	74	74	74	74	74	74	73	73	73	4
5	75	75	75	75	75	75	75	75	75	75	75	75	75	5
6	77	77	77	77	77	77	77	77	77	77	77	77	77	6
7	81	81	81	81	81	80	80	80	80	79	79	79	79	7
8	84	83	83	83	82	82	82	82	82	81	81	81	81	8
9	85	85	85	84	84	84	84	83	83	83	83	82	82	9
10	87	87	86	86	86	85	85	85	85	84	84	84	84	10
11	89	88	88	88	87	87	87	86	86	86	86	85	85	11
12	90	90	89	89	89	88	88	88	88	87	87	87	86	12
13	92	91	91	90	90	90	89	89	89	89	88	88	88	13
14	93	93	92	92	92	91	91	90	90	90	89	89	89	14
15	94	94	93	93	93	93	92	92	92	91	91	91	90	15
16	96	95	95	94	94	94	93	93	93	93	92	92	92	16
17	97	97	97	96	96	95	95	94	94	94	93	93	93	17
18	99	99	98	98	97	97	96	96	95	95	94	94	94	18
19	101	100	100	99	99	99	98	98	97	97	96	96	95	19
20	103	102	102	101	101	100	100	99	99	98	98	98	97	20
21	104	104	104	103	103	102	102	101	101	100	100	99	99	21
22	106	106	105	105	105	104	104	103	103	102	102	101	101	22
23	108	108	107	107	106	106	105	105	105	104	104	103	103	23
24	110	110	109	109	109	108	108	107	107	106	105	105	105	24
25	113	112	112	111	110	110	110	109	109	108	108	107	107	25
26	115	115	114	114	113	113	113	112	111	111	110	110	109	26
27	117	117	116	116	116	116	115	115	114	114	113	113	112	27
28	119	118	118	118	118	117	117	117	117	116	116	116	115	28
29	121	121	121	120	120	119	119	119	119	118	118	118	117	29
30	124	124	124	123	123	123	122	122	122	121	121	120	120	30
31	128	127	127	127	127	126	126	126	125	125	125	124	124	31
32				130	130	130	130	130	130	130	129	129	129	129	32
33														33
34	\multicolumn{13}{c}{Award >130 for all scores in this area}													34
35–40														35–40
	7:3	7:4	7:5	7:6	7:7	7:8	7:9	7:10	7:11	8:0	8:1	8:2	8:3	

Raw score	8:4	8:5	8:6	8:7	8:8	8:9	8:10	8:11	9:0	9:1	9:2	9:3	9:4	Raw score
					Age in years and completed months									
1														1
2					Award <70 for all scores in this area									2
3														3
4	71	71	71	71	70	70	70	70	70	70	70	70	70	4
5	73	73	73	73	72	72	72	72	72	72	72	72	72	5
6	75	75	75	75	75	75	75	75	75	75	75	75	75	6
7	77	77	77	77	77	77	77	76	76	76	76	76	76	7
8	79	79	79	79	79	79	79	79	79	79	79	78	78	8
9	81	81	80	80	80	80	80	80	80	80	80	79	79	9
10	82	82	82	82	81	81	81	81	81	81	81	80	80	10
11	83	83	83	83	83	82	82	82	82	82	82	82	81	11
12	85	85	84	84	84	84	83	83	83	83	83	83	82	12
13	86	86	86	85	85	85	85	84	84	84	84	84	84	13
14	87	87	87	87	86	86	86	86	85	85	85	85	85	14
15	89	88	88	88	88	87	87	87	87	86	86	86	86	15
16	90	90	89	89	89	88	88	88	88	88	87	87	87	16
17	91	91	91	90	90	90	89	89	89	89	88	88	88	17
18	93	92	92	92	91	91	91	90	90	90	89	89	89	18
19	94	93	93	93	93	92	92	92	91	91	91	90	90	19
20	95	94	94	94	94	93	93	93	93	92	92	92	91	20
21	97	96	96	95	95	94	94	94	94	93	93	93	93	21
22	98	98	98	97	97	96	96	95	95	94	94	94	93	22
23	100	100	99	99	98	98	97	97	97	96	96	95	95	23
24	102	102	101	101	100	100	99	99	98	98	97	97	97	24
25	104	104	103	103	102	102	101	101	100	100	99	99	98	25
26	106	106	105	105	104	104	104	103	102	102	101	101	100	26
27	109	108	108	107	107	106	105	105	105	104	104	103	102	27
28	111	111	110	110	109	109	108	108	107	106	106	105	105	28
29	115	114	114	113	112	112	111	110	110	109	109	108	107	29
30	117	117	116	116	116	115	115	114	113	113	112	111	110	30
31	119	119	119	118	118	118	117	117	117	116	116	115	114	31
32	124	123	123	122	122	121	121	120	120	119	119	118	118	32
33	128	128	128	127	127	127	126	126	125	125	124	124	123	33
34													130	34
35–40					Award >130 for all scores in this area									35–40
	8:4	8:5	8:6	8:7	8:8	8:9	8:10	8:11	9:0	9:1	9:2	9:3	9:4	

PiRA 4 Autumn

Raw score	Age in years and completed months																	Raw score
	7:4	7:5	7:6	7:7	7:8	7:9	7:10	7:11	8:0	8:1	8:2	8:3	8:4	8:5	8:6	8:7	8:8	
1	76	75	74	73	72	72	72	71	71	71	70	70	70	70	70	70	70	1
2	82	81	80	79	78	78	77	77	76	76	76	75	75	74	74	74	73	2
3	86	85	84	83	82	82	81	80	80	79	79	78	78	78	77	77	77	3
4	89	88	88	87	86	85	84	83	83	82	82	81	81	80	80	79	79	4
5	92	91	90	89	89	88	87	86	86	85	84	84	83	83	82	82	81	5
6	95	94	93	92	91	90	90	89	89	88	88	87	86	86	85	85	84	6
7	98	97	96	96	95	94	93	93	92	91	91	90	90	89	88	88	88	7
8	100	99	98	98	97	96	95	95	94	93	92	92	91	91	90	90	89	8
9	102	101	100	99	99	98	97	96	96	95	94	94	93	92	92	91	91	9
10	103	102	102	101	100	100	99	98	97	97	96	95	95	94	93	93	92	10
11	104	103	103	102	102	101	100	100	99	98	98	97	96	96	95	94	94	11
12	105	105	104	104	103	103	102	101	101	100	99	99	98	97	97	96	95	12
13	106	106	105	105	104	104	104	103	102	102	101	101	100	99	99	98	97	13
14	108	108	107	107	107	106	106	105	105	104	103	103	102	102	101	101	100	14
15	110	109	109	108	108	107	107	106	106	105	105	104	104	103	103	102	101	15
16	111	110	110	109	109	108	108	107	107	106	106	105	105	104	104	103	103	16
17	112	112	111	111	110	110	109	108	108	107	107	106	106	106	105	104	104	17
18	113	113	112	112	111	111	110	110	109	109	108	108	107	107	106	106	105	18
19	115	114	114	113	113	112	112	111	111	110	109	109	108	108	107	107	106	19
20	117	116	115	114	114	114	113	113	112	112	111	111	110	110	109	109	108	20
21	119	118	118	117	117	116	116	115	115	114	114	113	112	112	111	111	110	21
22	120	119	119	119	118	118	117	117	116	115	115	114	114	113	113	112	112	22
23	121	121	121	120	120	119	119	118	118	117	116	116	115	115	114	114	113	23
24	123	123	122	122	121	121	120	120	119	119	118	118	117	116	116	115	115	24
25	124	124	124	123	123	122	122	121	121	120	120	119	119	118	118	117	116	25
26	127	126	126	125	124	124	124	123	123	122	122	121	121	120	119	119	118	26
27	130	129	128	128	127	127	126	126	126	125	125	124	125	124	123	122	121	27
28										130	129	129	128	127	126	125	125	28
29															130	129	128	29
30																		30
31							Award >130 for all scores in this area											31
32																		32
33–40																		33–40
	7:4	7:5	7:6	7:7	7:8	7:9	7:10	7:11	8:0	8:1	8:2	8:3	8:4	8:5	8:6	8:7	8:8	

Raw score	8:9	8:10	8:11	9:0	9:1	9:2	9:3	9:4	9:5	9:6	9:7	9:8	9:9	9:10	9:11	10:0	Raw score
								Age in years and completed months									
1								Award <70 for all scores in this area									1
2	73	73	73	72	72	72	72	72	72	71	71	71	71	71	71	71	2
3	76	76	76	76	75	75	75	75	74	74	74	74	74	73	73	73	3
4	79	78	78	78	77	77	77	77	77	76	76	76	76	76	76	75	4
5	81	80	80	80	79	79	79	79	78	78	78	78	77	77	77	77	5
6	84	83	83	83	82	81	81	81	80	80	80	80	79	79	79	79	6
7	87	86	86	85	85	84	84	84	83	83	83	82	82	82	81	81	7
8	89	88	88	87	87	86	86	85	85	84	84	84	83	83	83	82	8
9	90	90	89	89	88	88	88	87	87	86	86	85	85	84	84	84	9
10	92	91	91	90	90	89	89	88	88	88	87	87	86	86	86	85	10
11	93	92	92	91	91	91	90	90	89	89	89	88	88	88	87	87	11
12	95	94	93	93	92	92	91	91	90	90	90	89	89	89	88	88	12
13	97	96	95	95	94	94	93	93	92	92	91	91	90	90	90	89	13
14	99	99	98	97	97	96	96	95	95	94	93	93	92	92	92	91	14
15	101	100	99	99	98	98	97	96	96	95	95	94	94	93	93	92	15
16	102	102	101	100	100	99	98	98	97	97	96	96	95	95	94	94	16
17	103	103	102	102	101	100	100	99	99	98	97	97	96	96	95	95	17
18	104	104	103	103	102	102	101	101	100	99	99	98	98	97	97	96	18
19	106	105	105	104	103	103	103	102	101	101	100	100	99	98	98	97	19
20	107	107	106	106	105	105	104	103	103	102	102	101	101	100	100	99	20
21	109	109	108	108	107	107	106	106	105	104	104	103	103	102	102	101	21
22	111	110	110	109	108	108	107	107	106	106	105	105	104	103	103	103	22
23	112	112	111	111	110	109	109	108	107	107	106	106	105	105	104	104	23
24	114	113	113	112	111	111	110	109	109	108	107	107	107	106	105	105	24
25	116	115	114	114	113	112	112	111	110	110	109	108	108	107	107	106	25
26	117	117	116	115	115	114	114	113	112	111	111	110	109	108	108	107	26
27	121	120	119	119	118	117	117	116	115	114	113	113	112	111	110	109	27
28	124	123	123	122	121	120	120	119	118	117	116	116	115	114	113	112	28
29	127	127	125	125	124	123	122	122	121	120	119	118	117	116	115	115	29
30			130	129	128	127	126	125	124	123	122	121	120	119	118	117	30
31							130	129	127	126	125	124	123	122	121	120	31
32													130	128	126	125	32
33–40								Award >130 for all scores in this area									33–40
	8:9	8:10	8:11	9:0	9:1	9:2	9:3	9:4	9:5	9:6	9:7	9:8	9:9	9:10	9:11	10:0	

PiRA 4 Spring

Raw score	8:0	8:1	8:2	8:3	8:4	8:5	8:6	8:7	8:8	8:9	8:10	8:11	9:0	Raw score
1														1
2							Award <70 for all scores in this area							2
3	70	70	70	70	70									3
4	73	73	73	73	73	72	72	72	72	72	72	72	72	4
5	77	77	77	76	76	76	76	76	76	76	76	76	76	5
6	80	80	79	79	79	79	79	78	78	78	78	78	78	6
7	82	82	82	81	81	81	81	81	81	80	80	80	80	7
8	84	83	83	83	83	83	82	82	82	82	82	82	82	8
9	85	85	85	84	84	84	84	84	83	83	83	83	83	9
10	87	87	86	86	86	86	85	85	85	85	84	84	84	10
11	89	88	88	88	87	87	87	87	86	86	86	86	85	11
12	90	90	90	90	89	89	89	88	88	88	87	87	87	12
13	92	91	91	91	91	90	90	90	90	89	89	89	88	13
14	93	93	92	92	92	91	91	91	91	91	90	90	90	14
15	95	94	94	94	93	93	92	92	92	92	91	91	91	15
16	96	96	95	95	95	94	94	94	93	93	93	92	92	16
17	97	97	97	96	96	96	95	95	95	94	94	94	93	17
18	99	98	98	98	97	97	97	96	96	96	95	95	95	18
19	100	99	99	99	99	99	98	98	97	97	97	96	96	19
20	102	102	102	101	101	101	100	100	99	99	99	98	98	20
21	104	103	103	102	102	102	101	101	101	100	100	100	99	21
22	105	105	104	104	103	103	103	102	102	102	101	101	101	22
23	107	107	106	106	105	105	104	104	103	103	102	102	102	23
24	109	108	108	107	107	106	106	105	105	104	104	103	103	24
25	110	110	109	109	109	108	108	107	107	106	106	105	105	25
26	112	111	111	111	110	110	109	109	108	108	107	107	106	26
27	113	113	112	112	112	111	111	110	110	110	109	109	108	27
28	115	115	114	114	113	113	112	112	111	111	111	110	110	28
29	117	117	116	116	115	115	114	113	113	112	112	112	111	29
30	119	119	118	118	117	117	116	115	115	114	114	113	113	30
31	122	121	121	120	119	119	118	118	117	116	116	115	115	31
32	125	124	124	123	122	122	121	120	119	119	118	118	117	32
33	128	128	127	126	125	124	124	123	122	122	121	120	119	33
34				130	129	128	127	126	126	125	124	123	123	34
35								130	129	129	128	127	126	35
36													130	36
37														37
38				Award >130 for all scores in this area										38
39														39
40														40
	8:0	8:1	8:2	8:3	8:4	8:5	8:6	8:7	8:8	8:9	8:10	8:11	9:0	

Raw score	Age in years and completed months													Raw score
	9:1	9:2	9:3	9:4	9:5	9:6	9:7	9:8	9:9	9:10	9:11	10:0	10:1	
1														1
2					Award <72 for all scores in this area									2
3														3
4	72	72	72	72	72	72	72	72	72	72	72	72	72	4
5	76	76	75	75	75	75	75	75	75	75	75	75	75	5
6	78	78	77	77	77	77	77	77	77	77	77	77	77	6
7	80	80	79	79	79	79	79	79	79	79	78	78	78	7
8	81	81	81	81	81	81	81	81	80	80	80	80	80	8
9	83	82	82	82	82	82	82	82	82	82	81	81	81	9
10	84	84	84	83	83	83	83	83	83	83	82	82	82	10
11	85	85	85	85	84	84	84	84	84	84	83	83	83	11
12	87	86	86	86	86	85	85	85	85	85	85	84	84	12
13	88	88	87	87	87	87	86	86	86	86	86	86	85	13
14	90	89	89	89	88	88	88	88	87	87	87	87	86	14
15	91	90	90	90	90	90	89	89	89	88	88	88	88	15
16	92	91	91	91	91	91	90	90	90	90	89	89	89	16
17	93	93	92	92	92	92	91	91	91	91	91	90	90	17
18	94	94	94	93	93	93	92	92	92	92	91	91	91	18
19	96	96	95	95	95	94	94	94	94	93	93	93	92	19
20	98	98	97	97	97	96	96	96	96	95	95	95	94	20
21	99	99	98	98	98	97	97	97	97	96	96	96	95	21
22	100	100	100	99	99	99	98	98	98	97	97	97	97	22
23	101	101	101	100	100	100	99	99	99	98	98	98	98	23
24	103	102	102	102	101	101	101	100	100	100	99	99	99	24
25	104	104	103	103	102	102	102	101	101	101	100	100	100	25
26	106	105	105	104	104	103	103	103	102	102	102	101	101	26
27	108	107	107	106	106	105	105	104	104	103	103	102	102	27
28	109	109	108	108	107	107	106	106	105	105	104	104	103	28
29	111	110	110	110	109	109	108	108	107	107	106	106	105	29
30	112	112	112	111	111	110	110	109	109	108	108	107	107	30
31	114	114	113	113	112	112	111	111	110	110	110	109	109	31
32	116	116	115	115	114	114	113	112	112	112	111	111	110	32
33	119	118	118	117	116	116	115	115	114	113	113	112	112	33
34	122	121	120	119	119	118	118	117	116	116	115	114	114	34
35	125	124	123	123	122	121	120	120	119	118	117	117	116	35
36	129	128	127	126	125	124	124	123	122	121	120	120	119	36
37					130	129	128	127	126	125	124	123	122	37
38									130	129	128	127	126	38
39					Award >130 for all scores in this area								130	39
40														40
	9:1	9:2	9:3	9:4	9:5	9:6	9:7	9:8	9:9	9:10	9:11	10:0	10:1	

PiRA 4 Summer

Raw score	8:3	8:4	8:5	8:6	8:7	8:8	8:9	8:10	8:11	9:0	9:1	9:2	9:3	Raw score
					Age in years and completed months									
1					Award <70 for all scores in this area									1
2	71	71	70	70										2
3	74	74	73	73	72	72	71	71	70	70				3
4	77	77	76	76	75	74	74	73	73	72	72	71	71	4
5	80	80	79	78	78	77	77	76	76	75	74	74	73	5
6	83	82	82	81	80	80	79	79	78	77	77	76	76	6
7	85	85	84	83	83	82	82	81	80	80	79	79	78	7
8	87	86	86	85	85	85	84	83	83	82	82	81	81	8
9	89	88	88	87	87	86	86	85	85	85	84	83	83	9
10	90	90	89	89	88	88	87	87	87	86	86	85	85	10
11	92	91	91	90	90	90	89	89	88	88	87	87	86	11
12	93	92	92	92	91	91	91	90	90	89	89	88	88	12
13	94	94	93	93	93	92	92	91	91	91	90	90	90	13
14	95	95	95	94	94	93	93	93	92	92	91	91	91	14
15	97	96	96	95	95	95	94	94	93	93	93	92	92	15
16	98	98	97	97	96	96	95	95	95	94	94	94	93	16
17	100	99	99	98	98	97	97	96	96	95	95	95	94	17
18	101	101	100	100	99	99	98	98	97	97	96	96	95	18
19	103	102	102	101	101	100	99	99	98	98	98	97	97	19
20	104	104	103	103	102	102	101	101	100	99	99	98	98	20
21	106	105	105	104	104	103	103	102	102	101	100	100	99	21
22	107	107	106	105	105	104	104	103	103	103	102	102	101	22
23	109	108	108	107	106	106	105	105	104	104	103	103	103	23
24	112	111	110	110	109	109	108	107	107	106	106	105	105	24
25	114	113	113	112	112	111	110	110	109	108	108	107	107	25
26	116	115	114	114	113	113	112	111	111	110	109	109	108	26
27	119	118	117	116	115	114	114	113	113	112	111	111	110	27
28	122	121	120	119	118	116	115	115	114	114	113	113	112	28
29	125	124	123	122	121	120	119	117	116	115	115	114	114	29
30	129	128	127	125	124	123	122	121	120	118	117	116	115	30
31				129	128	127	125	124	123	122	121	119	118	31
32							129	128	127	125	124	123	122	32
33										129	128	127	125	33
34													130	34
35														35
36				Award >130 for all scores in this area										36
37														37
38														38
39														39
40														40
	8:3	8:4	8:5	8:6	8:7	8:8	8:9	8:10	8:11	9:0	9:1	9:2	9:3	

Raw score	Age in years and months													Raw score
	9:4	9:5	9:6	9:7	9:8	9:9	9:10	9:11	10:0	10:1	10:2	10:3	10:4	
1														1
2					Award <70 for all scores in this area									2
3														3
4	71	70	70											4
5	73	73	72	72	71	71	70	70	70					5
6	75	75	74	74	74	73	73	72	72	71	71	71	70	6
7	78	77	77	76	76	75	75	75	74	74	73	73	72	7
8	80	80	79	79	78	78	77	77	76	76	75	75	75	8
9	82	82	81	81	80	80	79	79	78	78	77	77	77	9
10	84	84	83	83	82	82	81	81	80	80	79	79	78	10
11	86	86	85	85	84	84	83	83	82	82	81	81	80	11
12	87	87	87	86	86	85	85	85	84	84	83	83	82	12
13	89	89	88	88	87	87	87	86	86	85	85	85	84	13
14	90	90	90	89	89	88	88	88	87	87	86	86	86	14
15	92	91	91	91	90	90	89	89	89	88	88	87	87	15
16	93	92	92	92	91	91	91	90	90	90	89	89	88	16
17	94	94	93	93	92	92	92	91	91	91	90	90	90	17
18	95	95	94	94	94	93	93	92	92	92	91	91	91	18
19	96	96	95	95	95	94	94	94	93	93	93	92	92	19
20	97	97	97	96	96	95	95	95	94	94	94	93	93	20
21	99	98	98	97	97	97	96	96	95	95	95	94	94	21
22	100	100	99	99	98	98	97	97	97	96	96	95	95	22
23	102	102	101	100	100	99	99	98	98	97	97	97	96	23
24	104	104	103	103	102	102	101	101	100	100	99	99	98	24
25	106	106	105	105	104	104	103	103	102	102	101	101	100	25
26	108	107	107	106	105	105	104	104	104	103	103	102	102	26
27	109	109	108	108	107	106	106	105	105	104	104	103	103	27
28	111	110	110	109	109	108	108	107	106	106	105	105	104	28
29	113	112	112	111	110	110	109	109	108	107	107	106	106	29
30	115	114	114	113	112	112	111	110	110	109	108	108	107	30
31	117	116	115	115	114	113	113	112	112	111	110	110	109	31
32	121	119	118	117	116	115	115	114	113	113	112	111	111	32
33	124	123	122	121	119	118	117	116	115	115	114	113	113	33
34	128	127	125	124	123	122	120	119	118	117	116	115	114	34
35			130	128	127	125	124	123	122	120	119	118	117	35
36						130	128	127	125	124	123	122	120	36
37								130	128	127	125	124		37
38												130	128	38
39					Award >130 for all scores in this area									39
40														40
	9:4	9:5	9:6	9:7	9:8	9:9	9:10	9:11	10:0	10:1	10:2	10:3	10:4	

PiRA 5 Autumn

Raw score	\	\	\	\	\	\	Age in years and completed months	\	\	\	\	\	\	\	\	\	Raw score
	8:5	8:6	8:7	8:8	8:9	8:10	8:11	9:0	9:1	9:2	9:3	9:4	9:5	9:6	9:7	9:8	
1	75	73	70	70						Award <70 for all scores in this area							1
2	82	79	76	74	72	71	70	70	70								2
3	87	85	83	80	79	77	76	76	75	74	73	72	72	72	71	71	3
4	90	88	87	85	83	81	80	79	78	77	76	76	75	75	74	73	4
5	92	91	90	88	87	85	83	82	81	80	79	78	77	77	76	76	5
6	94	93	92	91	89	88	87	85	84	82	81	80	79	79	78	78	6
7	96	95	94	92	91	90	89	88	86	85	84	83	82	81	80	79	7
8	98	97	96	94	93	92	91	90	89	88	86	85	84	83	82	81	8
9	99	98	97	96	95	94	93	92	91	90	89	87	86	85	84	83	9
10	100	100	99	98	97	96	95	93	92	91	90	89	88	87	86	85	10
11	101	101	100	99	98	97	96	95	94	93	92	91	90	89	88	87	11
12	102	102	101	100	100	99	98	97	96	95	94	93	92	91	90	89	12
13	104	103	102	101	101	100	99	98	97	96	95	94	93	92	91	91	13
14	105	104	103	102	102	101	100	100	99	98	97	96	95	94	93	92	14
15	106	105	105	104	103	102	101	101	100	99	98	97	96	95	94	93	15
16	107	106	106	105	104	103	102	102	101	100	100	99	98	97	96	95	16
17	108	108	107	106	106	105	104	103	102	101	101	100	99	98	97	96	17
18	109	109	108	107	107	106	105	104	104	103	102	101	100	100	99	98	18
19	110	110	109	109	108	107	107	106	105	104	103	102	101	101	100	99	19
20	111	111	110	110	109	108	108	107	106	106	105	104	103	102	101	101	20
21	113	112	112	111	110	110	109	108	108	107	106	105	104	103	102	102	21
22	114	113	113	112	112	111	110	110	109	108	107	107	106	105	104	103	22
23	115	115	114	113	113	112	112	111	110	109	109	108	107	106	105	105	23
24	116	116	115	115	114	114	113	112	112	111	110	109	109	108	107	106	24
25	118	117	117	116	116	115	114	114	113	112	112	111	110	109	108	108	25
26	119	118	118	117	117	116	116	115	115	114	113	112	112	111	110	109	26
27	120	120	119	119	118	118	117	117	116	116	115	114	113	112	112	111	27
28	122	121	121	120	120	119	119	118	118	117	117	116	115	114	114	113	28
29	123	123	122	122	122	121	121	120	119	119	118	118	117	116	115	115	29
30	125	124	124	124	123	123	122	122	121	121	120	119	119	118	117	117	30
31	126	126	125	125	125	125	124	124	123	123	122	122	121	120	120	119	31
32	127	127	127	127	126	126	126	126	125	125	124	124	123	123	122	122	32
33	128	128	128	128	128	128	127	127	127	127	126	126	126	125	125	124	33
34	129	129	129	129	129	129	129	129	128	128	128	128	128	127	127	127	34
35					130	130	130	130	130	130	130	130	130	129	129	129	35
36																	36
37																	37
38																	38
39							Award >130 for all scores in this area										39
40																	40
	8:5	8:6	8:7	8:8	8:9	8:10	8:11	9:0	9:1	9:2	9:3	9:4	9:5	9:6	9:7	9:8	

Raw score	Age in years and completed months																Raw score
	9:9	9:10	9:11	10:0	10:1	10:2	10:3	10:4	10:5	10:6	10:7	10:8	10:9	10:10	10:11	11:0	
1																	1
2				Award <70 for all scores in this area													2
3	71	70	70	70	70	70	70	70	70								3
4	73	73	72	72	72	72	71	71	71	71	71	71	71	70	70	70	4
5	75	75	75	74	74	73	73	73	73	72	72	72	72	72	72	71	5
6	77	77	76	76	76	75	75	75	74	74	74	73	73	73	73	73	6
7	79	78	78	77	77	77	76	76	76	75	75	75	75	74	74	74	7
8	80	80	79	79	78	78	78	77	77	77	76	76	76	75	75	75	8
9	82	82	81	80	80	79	79	78	78	78	77	77	77	76	76	76	9
10	84	84	83	82	81	81	80	80	79	79	78	78	78	77	77	77	10
11	86	85	85	84	83	82	81	81	80	80	80	79	79	78	78	78	11
12	88	87	86	85	85	84	83	82	82	81	81	80	80	79	79	79	12
13	90	89	88	87	86	85	85	84	83	83	82	81	81	80	80	80	13
14	91	90	89	89	88	87	86	85	85	84	83	83	82	82	81	81	14
15	92	92	91	90	89	88	88	87	86	85	85	84	84	83	82	82	15
16	94	93	92	91	91	90	89	88	88	87	86	86	85	84	84	83	16
17	96	95	94	93	92	91	90	90	89	88	88	87	86	86	85	84	17
18	97	96	95	94	93	92	92	91	90	89	89	88	87	87	86	86	18
19	98	98	97	96	95	94	93	92	91	91	90	89	89	88	87	87	19
20	100	99	98	97	96	95	94	93	93	92	91	90	90	89	89	88	20
21	101	100	99	99	98	97	96	95	94	93	92	92	91	90	90	89	21
22	102	101	101	100	99	98	97	96	95	94	94	93	92	91	91	90	22
23	104	102	102	101	100	99	99	98	97	96	95	94	93	92	92	91	23
24	105	104	103	102	101	101	100	99	98	97	96	95	95	94	93	92	24
25	107	106	105	104	103	102	101	100	100	99	98	97	96	95	94	93	25
26	108	107	106	105	104	103	102	101	101	100	99	98	97	96	95	95	26
27	110	109	108	107	106	105	104	103	102	101	100	100	99	98	97	96	27
28	112	111	110	109	108	107	106	105	103	102	101	101	100	99	98	97	28
29	114	113	112	111	110	109	108	107	105	104	103	102	101	100	100	99	29
30	116	115	114	113	112	111	110	108	107	106	105	104	103	102	101	100	30
31	118	117	116	115	114	113	112	111	109	108	107	106	105	103	102	101	31
32	121	120	119	118	117	116	115	113	112	111	109	108	107	105	104	103	32
33	124	123	122	121	120	119	118	117	115	114	112	111	109	108	106	105	33
34	126	126	125	125	124	123	122	120	119	118	116	114	112	110	109	107	34
35	129	129	128	128	127	127	126	125	124	123	121	119	117	115	112	110	35
36								130	130	130	129	128	126	123	119	116	36
37															128	126	37
38				Award >130 for all scores in this area													38
39																	39
40																	40
	9:9	9:10	9:11	10:0	10:1	10:2	10:3	10:4	10:5	10:6	10:7	10:8	10:9	10:10	10:11	11:0	

PiRA 5 Spring

Raw score	Age in years and completed months													Raw score
	9:0	9:1	9:2	9:3	9:4	9:5	9:6	9:7	9:8	9:9	9:10	9:11	10:0	
1														1
2					Award <70 for all scores in this area									2
3	72	72	72	71	71	71	71	71	71	71	71	71	70	3
4	78	76	75	74	74	73	73	73	73	73	73	73	73	4
5	86	84	82	81	80	79	78	77	77	77	76	76	76	5
6	91	89	87	85	84	83	82	81	80	80	79	79	78	6
7	94	92	91	89	88	87	86	85	84	83	82	82	81	7
8	97	97	95	94	93	92	91	90	88	87	86	85	84	8
9	99	98	97	96	95	94	93	92	91	90	89	87	87	9
10	100	100	98	98	97	96	95	94	93	92	91	90	89	10
11	102	101	100	99	98	97	96	95	94	93	93	92	91	11
12	103	102	101	100	99	98	98	97	96	95	94	93	93	12
13	104	103	102	102	101	100	99	98	97	96	96	95	94	13
14	105	104	104	103	102	101	100	99	98	98	97	96	95	14
15	106	105	105	104	103	102	101	101	100	99	98	97	97	15
16	107	106	106	105	104	104	103	102	101	100	99	98	98	16
17	108	107	107	106	105	105	104	103	102	101	101	100	99	17
18	109	108	108	107	106	106	105	104	103	103	102	101	100	18
19	110	109	109	108	107	107	106	105	105	104	103	102	102	19
20	112	111	111	110	110	109	108	107	107	106	105	104	104	20
21	113	112	112	111	111	110	109	108	108	107	106	105	105	21
22	114	114	113	112	112	111	111	110	109	108	107	107	106	22
23	115	115	114	114	113	112	112	111	110	110	109	108	107	23
24	117	116	116	115	114	114	113	112	112	111	110	109	108	24
25	119	118	117	116	116	115	114	114	113	112	111	111	110	25
26	120	119	119	118	117	117	116	115	114	113	113	112	111	26
27	121	121	120	120	119	119	118	117	116	115	114	113	112	27
28	123	122	122	121	121	120	120	119	118	117	116	115	114	28
29	124	124	123	123	122	122	121	121	120	119	118	117	116	29
30	126	125	125	124	124	124	123	123	122	121	121	120	119	30
31	128	127	127	127	126	126	125	124	124	123	123	122	121	31
32	130	129	129	129	128	128	127	127	126	126	125	124	124	32
33					130	130	130	129	129	129	128	128	127	33
34													130	34
35					Award >130 for all scores in this area									35
36														36
37														37
38														38
39														39
40														40
	9:0	9:1	9:2	9:3	9:4	9:5	9:6	9:7	9:8	9:9	9:10	9:11	10:0	

Raw score	Age in years and completed months													Raw score
	10:1	10:2	10:3	10:4	10:5	10:6	10:7	10:8	10:9	10:10	10:11	11:0	11:1	
1														1
2			Award <70 for all scores in this area											2
3	70	70	70	70	70	70	70	70	70	70	70	70	70	3
4	73	73	73	72	72	72	72	72	72	72	72	72	72	4
5	75	75	75	75	75	75	74	74	74	74	74	74	74	5
6	78	77	77	77	77	76	76	76	76	76	76	75	75	6
7	80	80	79	79	79	78	78	78	77	77	77	77	77	7
8	82	82	81	81	80	80	80	79	79	79	78	78	78	8
9	84	83	83	82	82	82	81	81	81	80	80	80	79	9
10	86	85	84	84	83	83	82	82	82	81	81	81	81	10
11	88	87	86	85	85	84	84	83	83	83	82	82	82	11
12	90	89	88	87	86	86	85	85	84	84	83	83	83	12
13	92	91	90	89	88	87	87	86	85	85	84	84	84	13
14	93	92	92	91	90	89	89	88	87	86	86	85	85	14
15	94	94	93	92	92	91	90	90	89	88	87	87	86	15
16	96	95	94	93	93	92	92	91	90	90	89	88	87	16
17	97	96	95	95	94	93	93	92	92	91	90	90	89	17
18	98	97	97	96	95	94	94	93	93	92	92	91	90	18
19	99	98	98	97	96	96	95	94	94	93	93	92	91	19
20	101	100	99	98	97	97	96	95	95	94	93	93	93	20
21	102	101	100	99	98	98	97	96	96	95	94	94	93	21
22	103	102	101	100	100	99	98	97	97	96	96	95	94	22
23	104	103	102	102	101	100	99	98	98	97	97	96	95	23
24	105	104	104	103	102	101	100	100	99	98	97	97	96	24
25	106	105	105	104	103	102	101	101	100	99	98	98	97	25
26	107	107	106	105	104	103	103	102	101	100	100	99	98	26
27	109	108	107	106	105	105	104	103	102	101	101	100	99	27
28	110	109	108	107	107	106	105	104	103	103	102	101	100	28
29	112	111	110	109	108	107	106	105	105	104	103	102	101	29
30	113	112	112	111	110	109	108	107	106	105	104	103	102	30
31	115	114	113	112	111	110	109	108	107	106	105	104	104	31
32	118	117	115	114	113	112	111	110	109	108	107	106	105	32
33	120	120	118	117	116	114	113	112	111	110	108	107	106	33
34	123	122	121	120	119	118	116	114	113	112	110	109	108	34
35	126	125	124	123	122	121	120	118	116	114	113	111	110	35
36	130	129	129	128	127	125	124	123	121	119	117	115	112	36
37								130	128	126	124	121	118	37
38														38
39				Award >130 for all scores in this area										39
40														40
	10:1	10:2	10:3	10:4	10:5	10:6	10:7	10:8	10:9	10:10	10:11	11:0	11:1	

PiRA 5 Summer

Raw score	9:3	9:4	9:5	9:6	9:7	9:8	9:9	9:10	9:11	10:0	10:1	10:2	10:3	Raw score
							Age in years and completed months							
1														1
2						Award <70 for all scores in this area								2
3														3
4	73	73	72	72	72	72	72	71	71	71	71	71	71	4
5	77	76	76	76	75	75	74	74	74	73	73	73	73	5
6	80	80	79	78	78	77	77	76	76	76	75	75	75	6
7	83	82	82	81	80	80	79	79	78	78	77	77	77	7
8	86	85	84	83	83	82	82	81	80	80	79	79	79	8
9	89	88	87	86	85	84	84	83	82	82	81	81	81	9
10	92	91	90	90	89	88	88	87	86	85	85	84	83	10
11	95	94	94	93	92	92	91	90	89	88	87	87	86	11
12	97	96	95	95	94	93	93	92	91	90	90	89	88	12
13	99	98	97	97	96	95	94	93	93	92	92	91	90	13
14	101	100	99	98	97	97	96	95	94	94	93	93	92	14
15	102	102	101	100	99	98	98	97	96	95	95	94	93	15
16	104	103	102	102	101	100	100	99	98	97	96	96	95	16
17	106	105	104	103	103	102	102	101	100	99	98	98	97	17
18	108	108	107	107	106	105	104	103	103	102	102	101	100	18
19	110	109	109	108	107	107	106	105	104	104	103	102	102	19
20	112	111	110	109	109	108	108	107	106	105	105	104	103	20
21	114	113	112	111	110	110	109	108	108	107	106	106	105	21
22	116	115	114	113	113	112	111	110	109	109	108	107	106	22
23	118	117	116	116	115	114	113	112	111	110	109	109	108	23
24	122	121	120	119	118	117	117	116	115	114	113	112	111	24
25	126	125	124	123	122	121	120	119	118	117	116	115	114	25
26	128	127	127	126	125	124	123	122	121	119	119	118	117	26
27		130	129	129	128	127	126	125	124	123	122	120	119	27
28						130	129	128	127	126	125	124	123	28
29								130	129	128	127	126	29
30													130	30
31														31
32						Award >130 for all scores in this area								32
33–40														33–40
	9:3	9:4	9:5	9:6	9:7	9:8	9:9	9:10	9:11	10:0	10:1	10:2	10:3	

Raw score	Age in years and completed months													Raw score
	10:4	10:5	10:6	10:7	10:8	10:9	10:10	10:11	11:0	11:1	11:2	11:3	11:4	
1														1
2						Award <70 for all scores in this area								2
3														3
4	71	71	70	70	70	70	70	70	70	70	70	70	70	4
5	73	72	72	72	72	72	72	72	72	71	71	71	71	5
6	75	74	74	74	74	74	73	73	73	73	73	73	73	6
7	77	76	76	76	75	75	75	75	75	74	74	74	74	7
8	78	78	78	77	77	77	77	76	76	76	76	75	75	8
9	80	80	79	79	79	78	78	78	77	77	77	77	77	9
10	83	82	82	81	81	80	80	80	80	79	79	79	78	10
11	85	85	84	84	83	83	82	82	82	81	81	81	80	11
12	87	87	86	85	85	84	84	83	83	83	82	82	82	12
13	89	89	88	87	87	86	85	85	84	84	84	83	83	13
14	91	91	90	89	88	88	87	87	86	86	85	85	84	14
15	93	92	92	91	90	90	89	88	88	87	87	86	86	15
16	94	94	93	93	92	91	91	90	89	89	88	88	87	16
17	97	96	95	95	94	94	93	93	92	91	91	90	89	17
18	99	98	98	97	96	96	95	94	94	93	93	92	92	18
19	101	100	100	99	98	97	97	96	95	94	94	93	93	19
20	102	102	101	100	100	99	98	97	97	96	95	95	94	20
21	104	103	103	102	101	101	100	99	98	98	97	96	96	21
22	106	105	104	103	103	102	101	101	100	99	98	98	97	22
23	107	107	106	105	104	103	103	102	102	101	100	99	99	23
24	110	109	108	108	107	106	105	105	104	103	102	102	101	24
25	113	112	111	110	109	109	108	107	106	106	105	104	103	25
26	116	115	114	113	112	110	110	109	108	107	107	106	105	26
27	118	117	116	115	114	113	112	111	110	109	108	108	107	27
28	121	120	119	118	117	116	115	114	112	111	110	109	109	28
29	125	124	122	121	120	119	118	116	115	114	113	112	111	29
30	129	127	127	126	125	124	122	121	119	118	117	115	113	30
31							130	128	127	125	124	122	120	31
32			Award >130 for all scores in this area							130	129	127	125	32
33–40														33–40
	10:4	10:5	10:6	10:7	10:8	10:9	10:10	10:11	11:0	11:1	11:2	11:3	11:4	

Raw score	Age in years and completed months																Raw score
	9:5	9:6	9:7	9:8	9:9	9:10	9:11	10:0	10:1	10:2	10:3	10:4	10:5	10:6	10:7	10:8	
1																	1
2																	2
3					Award <70 for all scores in this area												3
4																	4
5	72	72	72	71	71	71	71	71	71	71	71	71	71	70	70	70	5
6	75	75	75	74	74	74	74	74	74	74	74	74	74	73	73	73	6
7	80	79	78	78	77	77	77	77	76	76	76	76	76	75	75	75	7
8	83	82	82	81	80	80	79	79	79	78	78	78	77	77	77	77	8
9	86	85	85	84	83	82	82	81	81	80	80	80	79	79	79	78	9
10	88	87	86	86	85	85	84	84	83	83	82	82	81	81	80	80	10
11	89	89	88	88	87	87	86	86	85	85	84	84	83	83	82	82	11
12	91	90	90	89	89	88	88	87	87	86	86	85	85	84	84	84	12
13	93	92	91	91	90	90	89	88	88	88	87	87	86	86	85	85	13
14	94	93	93	92	92	91	90	90	89	89	88	88	88	87	87	86	14
15	96	95	94	94	93	93	92	91	91	90	90	89	89	88	88	88	15
16	98	97	96	95	95	94	93	93	92	92	91	91	90	90	89	89	16
17	99	99	98	97	96	96	95	94	94	93	93	92	91	91	90	90	17
18	101	100	100	99	98	98	97	96	95	94	94	93	93	92	92	91	18
19	102	102	101	101	100	99	99	98	97	96	96	95	94	94	93	93	19
20	104	103	103	102	102	101	100	100	99	98	97	97	96	95	94	94	20
21	105	105	104	104	103	102	102	101	101	100	99	99	98	97	96	95	21
22	107	106	106	105	104	104	103	103	102	102	101	100	100	99	98	97	22
23	109	108	108	107	106	105	105	104	104	103	102	102	101	101	100	99	23
24	111	110	110	109	108	107	107	106	105	105	104	103	103	102	102	101	24
25	113	112	112	111	110	109	109	108	107	106	106	105	104	104	103	102	25
26	115	115	114	113	112	112	111	110	109	109	108	107	106	105	105	104	26
27	118	117	116	115	115	114	113	112	112	111	110	109	108	108	107	106	27
28	121	120	119	119	118	117	116	115	114	113	113	112	111	110	109	108	28
29	123	122	122	121	120	120	119	118	117	116	115	114	114	113	112	111	29
30	125	125	124	124	123	122	122	121	120	120	119	118	117	116	115	114	30
31	128	127	127	126	126	125	124	124	123	123	122	121	120	120	119	117	31
32	130	130	129	129	128	128	127	127	126	125	125	124	123	123	122	121	32
33							130	130	129	129	128	127	127	126	125	125	33
34													130	130	129	129	34
35																	35
36																	36
37					Award >130 for all scores in this area												37
38																	38
39																	39
40																	40
	9:5	9:6	9:7	9:8	9:9	9:10	9:11	10:0	10:1	10:2	10:3	10:4	10:5	10:6	10:7	10:8	

Raw score	10:9	10:10	10:11	11:0	11:1	11:2	11:3	11:4	11:5	11:6	11:7	11:8	11:9	11:10	11:11	12:0	Raw score
1																	1
2																	2
3					Award <70 for all scores in this area												3
4																	4
5	70	70	70	70	70	70	70	70	70	70	70	70	70	70	70	70	5
6	73	73	73	73	73	73	73	73	73	73	73	73	73	73	73	73	6
7	75	75	75	75	75	75	75	75	74	74	74	74	74	74	74	74	7
8	77	76	76	76	76	76	76	76	76	76	75	75	75	75	75	75	8
9	78	78	78	78	77	77	77	77	77	77	77	76	76	76	76	76	9
10	80	79	79	79	79	79	78	78	78	78	78	78	77	77	77	77	10
11	81	81	81	80	80	80	80	79	79	79	79	79	78	78	78	78	11
12	83	83	82	82	82	81	81	81	80	80	80	80	80	79	79	79	12
13	85	84	84	83	83	83	82	82	82	81	81	81	81	80	80	80	13
14	86	86	85	85	85	84	84	83	83	83	82	82	82	81	81	81	14
15	87	87	86	86	86	85	85	85	84	84	84	83	83	83	82	82	15
16	88	88	87	87	87	86	86	86	85	85	85	85	84	84	84	83	16
17	89	89	89	88	88	87	87	87	86	86	86	86	85	85	85	84	17
18	91	90	90	89	89	89	88	88	87	87	87	86	86	86	86	85	18
19	92	91	91	90	90	90	89	89	88	88	88	87	87	87	87	86	19
20	93	93	92	92	91	91	90	90	89	89	89	88	88	88	87	87	20
21	95	94	94	93	93	92	92	91	91	90	90	89	89	89	88	88	21
22	96	96	95	94	94	93	93	92	92	91	91	90	90	90	89	89	22
23	98	98	97	96	95	95	94	94	93	93	92	92	91	91	90	90	23
24	100	100	99	98	97	96	96	95	94	94	93	93	92	92	91	91	24
25	102	101	101	100	99	98	98	97	96	95	95	94	93	93	93	92	25
26	103	103	102	102	101	100	99	99	98	97	96	96	95	94	94	93	26
27	105	105	104	103	103	102	101	100	100	99	98	97	97	96	95	94	27
28	107	107	106	105	104	104	103	102	101	101	100	99	99	98	97	96	28
29	110	109	108	107	106	105	105	104	103	103	102	101	100	100	99	98	29
30	113	112	111	110	109	108	107	106	105	104	104	103	102	101	101	100	30
31	116	115	114	113	112	111	110	109	108	107	106	105	104	103	103	102	31
32	120	119	118	117	116	114	113	112	111	110	109	108	107	105	105	104	32
33	124	123	122	121	120	119	118	116	115	114	112	111	110	109	107	106	33
34	128	127	126	125	124	123	122	121	120	119	117	115	114	112	111	110	34
35				130	129	128	127	126	125	124	123	121	120	118	116	114	35
36										130	129	128	126	125	123	121	36
37																130	37
38				Award >130 for all scores in this area													38
39																	39
40																	40
	10:9	10:10	10:11	11:0	11:1	11:2	11:3	11:4	11:5	11:6	11:7	11:8	11:9	11:10	11:11	12:0	

Raw score	Age in years and completed months													Raw score
	10:0	10:1	10:2	10:3	10:4	10:5	10:6	10:7	10:8	10:9	10:10	10:11	11:0	
1	70													1
2	73	72	71	71	70			Award <70 for all scores in this area						2
3	76	75	74	73	73	72	71	70	70					3
4	78	77	76	76	75	75	74	73	72	72	71	70	70	4
5	80	79	79	78	77	77	76	76	75	74	74	73	72	5
6	82	81	81	80	79	79	78	78	77	76	76	75	75	6
7	83	83	82	82	81	81	80	80	79	78	78	77	77	7
8	84	84	84	83	83	82	82	81	81	80	80	79	79	8
9	86	85	85	85	84	84	83	83	82	82	82	81	81	9
10	87	87	86	86	85	85	85	84	84	83	83	82	82	10
11	89	88	88	87	87	86	86	86	85	85	84	84	83	11
12	90	89	89	89	88	88	87	87	87	86	86	85	85	12
13	91	90	90	90	89	89	89	88	88	87	87	87	86	13
14	92	92	91	91	91	90	90	89	89	89	88	88	87	14
15	94	93	93	92	92	91	91	91	90	90	89	89	89	15
16	95	95	94	94	93	93	92	92	91	91	91	90	90	16
17	97	96	96	95	95	94	94	93	93	92	92	91	91	17
18	98	98	97	97	96	96	95	95	94	94	93	93	92	18
19	99	99	98	98	98	97	97	96	96	95	95	94	94	19
20	100	100	100	99	99	99	98	98	97	97	96	96	95	20
21	102	101	101	100	100	100	99	99	99	98	98	97	97	21
22	103	103	102	102	102	101	101	100	100	99	99	99	98	22
23	105	104	104	103	103	103	102	102	101	101	100	100	99	23
24	106	106	106	105	105	104	104	103	103	102	102	102	101	24
25	108	108	107	107	106	106	105	105	104	104	103	103	103	25
26	110	109	109	109	108	108	107	107	106	106	105	105	104	26
27	112	111	111	110	110	109	109	109	108	108	107	107	106	27
28	113	113	113	112	112	111	111	110	110	109	109	108	108	28
29	116	115	115	114	114	113	113	112	112	111	111	111	110	29
30	117	117	117	116	116	116	115	115	114	114	113	112	112	30
31	119	119	118	118	118	117	117	117	116	116	115	115	114	31
32	122	121	121	120	120	119	119	119	118	118	118	117	117	32
33	125	124	124	123	123	122	122	121	121	120	120	119	119	33
34	128	127	127	126	126	125	125	124	124	123	123	122	122	34
35			130	130	129	129	128	128	127	127	126	126	125	35
36											130	130	129	36
37														37
38			Award >130 for all scores in this area											38
39														39
40														40
	10:0	10:1	10:2	10:3	10:4	10:5	10:6	10:7	10:8	10:9	10:10	10:11	11:0	

Raw score	11:1	11:2	11:3	11:4	11:5	11:6	11:7	11:8	11:9	11:10	11:11	12:0	12:1	Raw score
					Age in years and completed months									
1														1
2						Award <70 for all scores in this area									2
3														3
4														4
5	72	71	70	70										5
6	74	73	73	72	71	71	70	70						6
7	76	76	75	74	74	73	73	72	71	71	70	70		7
8	78	78	77	76	76	75	75	74	74	73	72	72	71	8
9	80	79	79	78	78	77	77	76	76	75	75	74	73	9
10	82	81	81	80	80	79	79	78	78	77	76	76	75	10
11	83	83	82	82	81	81	80	80	79	79	78	78	77	11
12	84	84	83	83	83	82	82	81	81	81	80	80	79	12
13	86	85	85	84	84	83	83	83	82	82	82	81	81	13
14	87	87	86	86	85	85	84	84	84	83	83	82	82	14
15	88	88	87	87	87	86	86	85	85	84	84	84	83	15
16	89	89	89	88	88	88	87	87	86	86	85	85	84	16
17	91	90	90	89	89	89	88	88	88	87	87	86	86	17
18	92	91	91	91	90	90	89	89	89	88	88	88	87	18
19	93	93	92	92	92	91	91	90	90	89	89	89	88	19
20	95	94	94	93	93	92	92	92	91	91	90	90	89	20
21	96	96	95	95	94	94	93	93	92	92	92	91	91	21
22	98	97	97	96	96	96	95	94	94	93	93	93	92	22
23	99	99	98	98	98	97	97	96	96	95	95	94	94	23
24	100	100	100	99	99	98	98	98	97	97	96	96	95	24
25	102	102	101	101	100	100	99	99	99	98	98	97	97	25
26	104	103	103	102	102	101	101	100	100	99	99	99	98	26
27	106	105	105	104	103	103	103	102	102	101	100	100	100	27
28	107	107	107	106	105	105	104	104	103	103	102	102	101	28
29	110	109	108	108	107	107	106	106	105	105	104	104	103	29
30	112	111	111	110	110	109	108	108	107	107	106	106	105	30
31	114	113	113	112	112	111	111	110	110	109	108	108	107	31
32	116	116	115	115	114	114	113	112	112	111	111	110	110	32
33	118	118	118	117	117	116	116	115	115	114	113	113	112	33
34	121	121	120	119	119	119	118	118	117	117	116	116	115	34
35	125	124	124	123	123	122	121	121	120	119	119	118	118	35
36	129	128	128	127	127	126	125	125	124	123	123	122	121	36
37						130	130	129	129	128	127	127	126	37
38														38
39			Award >130 for all scores in this area											39
40														40
	11:1	11:2	11:3	11:4	11:5	11:6	11:7	11:8	11:9	11:10	11:11	12:0	12:1	

PiRA 6 Summer

Raw score	10:3	10:4	10:5	10:6	10:7	10:8	10:9	10:10	10:11	11:0	11:1	11:2	11:3	Raw score
1														1
2					Award <70 for all scores in this area									2
3														3
4														4
5	71	71	71	71	71	71	71	71	71	71	71	70	70	5
6	74	74	74	74	74	73	73	73	73	73	73	73	72	6
7	77	77	77	76	76	76	76	75	75	75	75	75	75	7
8	80	79	79	79	78	78	78	78	77	77	77	77	77	8
9	82	82	81	81	81	80	80	80	80	79	79	79	78	9
10	85	84	84	84	83	83	82	82	82	81	81	81	80	10
11	87	86	86	86	85	85	85	84	84	84	83	83	83	11
12	89	89	88	88	87	87	86	86	86	85	85	85	85	12
13	91	91	91	90	90	89	89	88	88	87	87	87	86	13
14	93	93	92	92	92	91	91	90	90	90	89	89	88	14
15	95	95	94	94	93	93	93	92	92	91	91	91	90	15
16	97	96	96	95	95	95	94	94	94	93	93	92	92	16
17	98	98	97	97	97	96	96	96	95	95	94	94	94	17
18	100	99	99	99	98	98	98	97	97	96	96	96	95	18
19	102	102	101	100	100	100	99	99	98	98	98	97	97	19
20	104	104	103	103	102	102	101	100	100	100	99	99	98	20
21	106	105	105	104	104	104	103	103	102	102	101	100	100	21
22	107	107	107	106	106	105	105	104	104	104	103	103	102	22
23	109	109	108	108	108	107	107	106	106	105	105	104	104	23
24	111	111	110	110	109	109	108	108	108	107	107	106	106	24
25	114	113	113	112	112	111	110	110	109	109	109	108	108	25
26	117	116	116	116	115	115	114	114	113	113	112	112	111	26
27	120	119	119	119	118	118	117	117	116	116	115	115	114	27
28	123	122	122	121	121	120	120	119	119	118	118	117	117	28
29	125	125	124	124	123	123	122	122	121	121	120	120	119	29
30	129	128	128	127	127	126	125	125	124	124	123	123	122	30
31				130	130	129	129	128	128	127	127	126	125	31
32											130	130	129	32
33														33
34					Award >130 for all scores in this area									34
35–40														35–40
	10:3	10:4	10:5	10:6	10:7	10:8	10:9	10:10	10:11	11:0	11:1	11:2	11:3	

Raw score	Age in years and completed months													Raw score
	11:4	11:5	11:6	11:7	11:8	11:9	11:10	11:11	12:0	12:1	12:2	12:3	12:4	
1														1
2														2
3					Award <70 for all scores in this area									3
4														4
5	70	70	70	70	70	70	70	70	70	70	70	70	70	5
6	72	72	72	72	72	72	72	72	72	72	72	71	71	6
7	74	74	74	74	74	74	74	73	73	73	73	73	73	7
8	76	76	76	76	76	75	75	75	75	75	75	75	75	8
9	78	78	78	78	77	77	77	77	77	77	76	76	76	9
10	80	80	80	79	79	79	79	79	78	78	78	78	78	10
11	82	82	82	81	81	81	80	80	80	80	80	79	79	11
12	84	84	84	83	83	83	82	82	82	81	81	81	81	12
13	86	86	85	85	85	85	84	84	84	83	83	83	82	13
14	88	87	87	87	86	86	86	85	85	85	85	84	84	14
15	90	90	89	89	88	88	87	87	87	86	86	86	86	15
16	92	91	91	91	90	90	89	89	89	88	88	87	87	16
17	93	93	92	92	92	91	91	91	90	90	90	89	89	17
18	95	95	94	94	93	93	93	92	92	92	91	91	91	18
19	96	96	96	95	95	95	94	94	94	93	93	92	92	19
20	98	98	97	97	96	96	96	95	95	95	94	94	94	20
21	100	99	99	98	98	98	97	97	97	96	96	95	95	21
22	102	101	100	100	100	99	99	98	98	98	97	97	97	22
23	104	103	103	102	102	101	101	100	100	99	99	98	98	23
24	105	105	105	104	104	103	103	102	102	101	101	100	100	24
25	107	107	106	106	105	105	105	104	104	103	103	102	102	25
26	111	110	110	109	109	108	108	107	107	106	106	105	104	26
27	114	113	113	112	112	111	110	110	109	109	108	108	107	27
28	116	116	115	115	114	114	113	113	112	111	111	110	109	28
29	119	118	118	117	117	116	115	115	114	114	113	113	112	29
30	122	121	120	120	119	119	118	117	117	116	116	115	115	30
31	125	124	124	123	122	122	121	120	120	119	119	118	117	31
32	129	128	127	127	126	125	125	124	123	123	122	121	121	32
33					130	129	129	128	127	127	126	125	124	33
34												130	129	34
35–40					Award >130 for all scores in this area									35–40
	11:4	11:5	11:6	11:7	11:8	11:9	11:10	11:11	12:0	12:1	12:2	12:3	12:4	